NOTHING LIKE
SUNSHINE

Ben Kamin

NOTHING LIKE SUNSHINE

A Story in the Aftermath
of the MLK Assassination

MICHIGAN STATE UNIVERSITY PRESS | EAST LANSING

⊖ The paper used in this publication meets the minimum requirements of ANSI/NISO
Z39.48-1992 (R 1997) (Permanence of Paper).

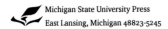 Michigan State University Press
East Lansing, Michigan 48823-5245

Printed and bound in the United States of America.

16 15 14 13 12 11 10   1 2 3 4 5 6 7 8 9 10

LIBRARY OF CONGRESS CATALOGING-IN-PUBLICATION DATA
Kamin, Ben.
Nothing like sunshine : a story in the aftermath of the MLK assassination / Ben Kamin.
p. cm.
Includes bibliographical references.
ISBN 978-0-87013-882-9 (pbk. : alk. paper) 1. Kamin, Ben. 2. Rabbis—United States—
Biography. 3. Fleetwood, Clifton. 4. African Americans—Relations with Jews. 5.
Woodward High School (Cincinnati, Ohio) 6. African American—Civil rights—History—
20th century. 7. Civil rights movements—United States—History—20th century. 8. United
States—Race relations. 9. Cincinnati (Ohio)—Race relations. I. Title.
BM755.K285A3 2010
296.092—dc22
[B]
2009049805

Cover and book design by Charlie Sharp, Sharp Designs, Lansing, Michigan

green Michigan State University Press is a member of the Green Press Initiative and is
press committed to developing and encouraging ecologically responsible publishing
INITIATIVE practices. For more information about the Green Press Initiative and the use of recycled paper
in book publishing, please visit www.greenpressinitiative.org.

Visit Michigan State University Press on the World Wide Web at *www.msupress.msu.edu*

It's for Audrey

Contents

NOTHING LIKE
SUNSHINE

Room B4

The Rev. Dr. Martin Luther King, Jr.'s body lay in the morgue of St. Joseph's Hospital in Memphis when I awoke in my bedroom, damp with sweat and worry. How far, I wondered, was the distance from Cincinnati to Memphis? Not far, I knew. Four hundred miles? Not so far. I was in the tenth grade, and slept uneasily with the images of corpses, guns, battles, and now a fallen preacher—although I was in the cozy sanctuary of my oak-shaded room with the little alcove for my desk that overlooked the quiet street. It was a reddish-brick house, Midwestern stock, with a narrow chimney—the dwelling solid and simple, introduced by a tiny railed stoop in front with three steps.

People had always touted my town, Cincinnati, as a Southern city, a would-be Atlanta, not at all like the starchy, flat dead-center Midwestern capital of Columbus, or the smoke-stacked, northeastern, urban-weary

Cleveland. Not in "Cincy," with the twang that was so often heard in casual conversation in the corner "Pony Keg" mini-marts. There you could buy snow cones, the daily *Cincinnati Enquirer*, Hudepohl beer, five-cent Ibold cigars, and Reds baseball trading cards. The city was bordered by the muddy green waters of the Ohio. The heavy migrant Appalachian population weighed in along with the humidity, especially in the Carthage, Hartwell, and Western Hills sections—which also yielded Pete Rose, the ultimate native scion, who had more hits than any baseball player ever but was ultimately banished from the game for his gambling habits.

Cincinnati: I remember the seven-year cycle of cicada locusts that left their eerie skeletal remains staring at us young boys from the stricken trunks of birch trees. And the presence of the Commonwealth of Kentucky and its booze-and-women clubs, forbidden haunts of "boondocks *noir*," cheap cigarettes and whiskey, in Newport and Covington and Erlanger—just across the steaming river from our grayish downtown and its Dixie Terminal Building. Yet I had a sense of place—obstinately patriotic, quite distinct—and a consciousness, that morning of April 5, 1968, of how the Ohio River naturally blended into the Mississippi, linking my civic coordinates to Memphis and my heart to the American story.

So I felt a certain proximity to what had happened the night before at the Lorraine Motel and wanted to put my head in my hands and just moan. But I trembled instead, cold flashes attacking my spine, and the image of the silenced preacher prone in his blood on the Lorraine walkway glaring in my eyes. Was I being selfish, at fifteen years of age, to feel cheated that I had never met Dr. King? Or was I just being reverent? I did not know which, although I did know that I was frightened.

I remembered when President John F. Kennedy was slain, less than five years earlier. The tiny Hebrew day school I then attended suddenly sent us home just before two o'clock—exactly when we would have concluded our day with the weekly all-classes welcoming of Sabbath. There would be no plastic mini-cups of grape juice, thin challah slices, lit candles, and sung blessings that Friday afternoon. I wouldn't have the opportunity to swoon over my willowy fellow sixth grader, Linda Gerstle, outside of the confined classroom, and in the cold sunshine of our modest playground behind the brown brick building. That was an unseasonably pleasant day, November 22, 1963. I scanned the front entranceway on Summit Road, and there was my mother in her gray Dodge Lancer with the push-button transmission. The breeze picked up and seemed to start howling and the skies turned dark as I sat in the seat next to her and realized that she was sobbing. The radio was not tuned for me to "Top 40" WSAI/1360 AM for the Crystals and Dionne Warwick. No, it was Clear Channel WLW 700, the Nation's Station, where there was news piped in from NBC spoken by hushed, urgent-sounding men about confusion and blood and crushed flowers and a young widow in Dallas, Texas.

We made our way, as we did every Friday afternoon, to pick up a twisted challah at the Avon Bakery on Reading Road. There, the narrow-waisted, kindly older ladies, clad in pink service dresses, were working dutifully and silently behind the counter, running poppy seed and regular loaves through the single slicing machine, handing over waxy bags to their customers while openly crying—as the radio on the shelf above the fruit pastry blasted the shocking dispatches from Dallas and Washington. Next to us stood Dr. Glanzberg, the sinewy orthodontist who had survived Treblinka and Dachau only eighteen years earlier, who worked on my braces while vigorously humming along with the Puccini operas that he piped into the office via WGUC-FM. Now he held onto his rye bread as if someone terrible was coming back again to take it away from him. He smiled at me in a crooked, forced way, and I saw trepidation in his eyes that told me something had been shaken from its foundations.

That was the beginning of everything as we came to know the 1960s, and it's hard to remember anything clearly before November 22, 1963. A wispy, eerie man named Lee Harvey Oswald, ex-Marine, alleged commie, Russian expatriate, came through the cathode ray of the black-and-white television set with the pronged antennae and click-click channel setter. We had real demons to fear and young men to bury, starting with the chestnut-haired president and hemorrhaging into thousands and thousands of peach-fuzzed soldiers who began to die for us in the jungles and rice paddies and fires of Vietnam.

Broadcast live on my luckless living room Zenith, a stocky TV-gangster look-a-like named Jack Ruby thrust himself out of the grainy crowd in the Dallas police garage and fired a pistol into the sweater of Lee Harvey Oswald that very Sunday afternoon, November 24, 1963. Suddenly, the government and policemen were no longer sacrosanct as we assumed they were, and nothing seemed as safe as we took for granted it would be. There was now "A Threat" out there. Violent death was abruptly an unwelcome companion in our thoughts. There was a new vulnerability; some (including me) thought of fleeing to Canada to avoid the inexplicable war. Race riots scorched everything the next several summers from Newark to Watts. Japanese cars and lavish bar mitzvah parties and Afros and bell-bottoms and condoms came through like the tide, and even Linda Gerstle went on to her life, and our innocent little crush upon each other was as distant and ethereal as the morning stars disappearing into the blazing light of a postmodernity that everyone feted but none of us really, truly welcomed.

• • • • •

April 5, 1968: It was Chet Huntley we watched the night before on NBC, breaking into the programming and announcing that "Martin Luther King was shot and killed tonight in Memphis." I immediately thought of Clifton Fleetwood, my friend at school since we had arrived there together, from different places, tenth months after the assassination of President Kennedy. And I thought of Clifton now, as the morning came to reveal the charred and smoking landscape of so many American cities. I had wanted to call Clifton the night before, in the wake of the terrible news, and certainly after the breathless reporters on NBC, CBS, and ABC began their dispatches about the rioting in Washington, DC, and elsewhere that went on all through the night. I had wanted to call Clifton, but realized, with a bit of shame, that I did not have his telephone number and had never actually phoned him since we first met in seventh grade three years previously. We played in the Woodward High School Marching Band together, ate lunch together from time to time at the edge of the socially segregated cafeteria on the top floor of the high school, ran through the halls of the cavernous building in mischief and glee, and ritualistically smoked Marlboro cigarettes behind toilet stalls and in the back of the basement band hall, Room B4. We skipped chemistry class together once a week or so and defiantly walked across the heavily trafficked Reading Road and into Swifton Shopping Center, the nation's first such shopping plaza, and gobbled corn dogs and root beer at the soda fountain of G. C. Murphy and Co. five-and-ten store. But I didn't have Clifton's telephone number, had only a vague idea of where he lived, assuming it was in the formerly Jewish and now predominantly black section of town called Avondale. This was where synagogues had been converted into Baptist churches, and former boutiques were now Aamco Transmission centers—in which grease-stained black men calibrated engine timing on Pontiacs and Studebakers and installed PCV valves. They balanced tires for middle-level white managers who locked their car doors promptly upon heading home to the Norwood, Bond Hill, and Kenwood sections of town. Wringing my hands, imagining Dr. King's almond eyes staring lifelessly up to the sky from the Lorraine balcony, I realized that my comradeship with Clifton Fleetwood was a daytime, Monday–Friday event, and included none of the secrets and the terrors that constitute a true friendship.

Clifton Fleetwood ("a Cadillac among men," he would describe himself) had been my indomitable crony from the second month of seventh grade, fall of 1964. I was still cowering in the halls in this urban behemoth of a high school, with grades seven through twelve, a great and strange multicultural patchwork of 3,600 students, and a labyrinth of hallways and crevices and orifices that—I learned quickly and brutally—were the stomping grounds of wandering thieves and thugs who, like bats, pounced upon innocent little seventh graders who had just matriculated from a cozy Hebrew day school of fifty-five monolithic tenderfoots. A grown man, an eleventh grader, with a steel-wool dark beard to frame his fierce, angry ebony face stood over me once while I lamely turned the combination of my locker. When I wheeled around, he promptly punched me in the throat and took off, along with his two chortling escorts. Why was I then surprised the next afternoon when I discovered the locker open, empty, ransacked, and filled with urine?

I had just completed two terms as president of the Yavneh Day School Junior Congregation and was not quite ready for this kind of cultural abrasion. My parents, normally militant and generally infallible, seemed helpless to come up with what to do, and my scoutmaster at Troop 265 of the Jewish Community Center could only tell me to be strong and show courage. "But don't even try to report it," he added. "They all look the same."

They didn't, not to me. Especially Clifton. I actually don't remember the exact circumstances of our meeting and talking for the first time, but I saw him from the beginning, amongst the drums and cymbals, in the back section of the octagonal Band Room adjacent to the band teacher's cramped office. Clifton, black, brash, skinny, and very musical, would eventually become the drum major of our Bulldogs Marching Band, with blue and white colors and black and white faces. Besides attempting to play the B-flat clarinet, I became the assistant drum major in due time, thanks largely to Clifton's proactive stance with the Southern-born-and-bred Mr. Raleigh Taylor. Taylor was the courtly, dark-haired director who wanted to be down there with us as much as he wanted to drink ink. Taylor, with deep-set blue eyes, his inner life still unrealized, actually a kindhearted man, sought the real world of concert music, and he certainly made it clear to us howling rhythm-assassins that he had only come to Cincinnati from Ft. Benning in Columbus, Georgia, to transition from the army, and that he wanted to be around a higher caliber of composition. That he was a man with a hungry soul was confirmed one day in our eighth-grade year when Clifton (of course) started the 1:40 P.M. class off by hushing us all and then ceremoniously swinging the door of Mr. Taylor's office wide open (with his own set of keys, naturally), revealing the conductor in deep occupation with the rod-thin and leggy Miss Armstrong, junior high English teacher and intermittent companion of our young, single, and noble leader.

"My, God, Mr. Taylor!" yelled Clifton Fleetwood, as every wind, brass, string, and percussion instrument exploded gleefully, a sarcastic cacophony there in the poorly ventilated chamber known as Room B4. The moment of triumphant anarchy, a typhoon of clapping and laughter, was blunted by

Mr. Taylor's sweeping recovery from the exposure. Standing up, gracefully buttoning his dark blazer, his lips quivering, throwing his thick hair back with his palms, gently directing the English teacher aside within the narrow space between his desk and the cubicle wall, the maestro marched to the doorway, glared at Clifton, and proclaimed:

"You all are so dumb that you wouldn't even comprehend. Clifton, see me after school."

But Clifton and Raleigh Taylor actually had a polite if tragic understanding, something resembling a reenacted antebellum relationship that the adult pursued without intended malice and the youngster acceded to with a political and ingrained social instinct. The fact that Raleigh Taylor was anything but an elitist would be proven over the next several decades while he taught music to myriad youngsters of all ages and backgrounds in the less-hectic confines of Harford County's public schools in Maryland. He packed his cherished trombone and was gone from the turbulent halls of Woodward High School by 1969.

But while there, the director liked my friend Clifton's good-natured assertiveness and his accomplished administrative skills. The truth is that Clifton *ran* the band while Taylor pined for his next opportunity to sub in the Cincinnati Symphony, or jam in one of the local jazz groups that drew him in. The results were that we actually *had* our treble and clef sheets, drum sticks, and reeds, and we gave off a decent sound on the open-air football field of our beloved Bulldogs while creating a formation to the beat of "*A pretty girl is like a melody . . .*"

Mr. Taylor never had to worry about launching the weekly Friday-morning pep-band marches around the school that began at 7:00 A.M. While the teacher sipped on coffee and ate Dunkin' Donuts from Swifton Center, Clifton was already there, having taken an even earlier city bus than usual from his stop, several miles south on Reading Road. He was clockwork in his band manifestation, and he set us up, clipping small bits of sheet music with nimble, long fingers into the slots above this one's trumpet and that one's saxophone and—on my happiest days—turning over his big bass drum to me while he led the way, animated, proud, and truly talented. Upon our return from the heady march and rally on behalf of our perennial Public High School League (PHSL) champions, who were in those days spearheaded by the future Michigan star and Rose Bowl standout Eddie Shuttlesworth (who played trombone for Clifton when football wasn't in season), we feasted upon a generous spread of the doughnuts quietly left behind by Raleigh Taylor. Dutifully, Clifton cleaned up the sugary, flaky crumbs after us, sponged the milk and coffee stains, discarded the teacher's morning *Enquirer* in the trash bin, and then locked the office with the same key that he used to intermittently dismay the doe-eyed Mr. Taylor. No, it was clear to me that the lily-white Taylor and the urban-black Fleetwood found common ground somewhere upon the landscape of high school practicalities and Southern sensibilities. If, for example, Clifton knew what the deal really was between the bandleader and the English teacher, he never divulged anything. And even when Clifton tested Mr. Taylor's temper on a particularly dreary afternoon, the teacher never delivered the ultimate punch of suspension or disenfranchisement upon his young protégé. Yes, even after the following exchange, on an afternoon when Taylor was trying to inspire us to successfully play Billy May's arrangement of "Serenade in Blue," Clifton survived.

TAYLOR: Everyone, stop. *Stop!* Clifton, what are you doing back there? What are you swallowing? I can see that you are swallowing something.

CLIFTON: I'm taking a aspirin, sir.

TAYLOR (*tapping his baton upon the music stand as though beating an animal*): Why are you taking *an* aspirin?

CLIFTON: Because the band give me a headache. (*General laughter*).

April 5, 1968: My father, an early riser, had already departed for his office at General Electric's large aerospace engineering center in suburban Evendale. My mother prepared for what would be a taut day of teaching at her school. I began my daily walk to Woodward, accompanied by my buddy and fellow junior historian, Steve Hirschberg. Steve waited by our side door on Bluefield Place in Roselawn, almost obediently, most mornings. We took our daily trek down to Losantiville Avenue, then a short right to Reading Road and the Roselawn Lutheran Church and its sappy aphorisms printed on the outdoor board ("Know Christ Today, Know Thyself Tomorrow"). Then it was uphill and south for a long block, past Marcy Greenbaum's house and our fantasies of the tight-boned and cheery drill-team majorette, past the "Red Barn" burger place where I worked on weekends, and on to Mel Abrams's Mobil gasoline station and car-repair center at the imposing intersection of Seymour and Reading roads. There, across the block, loomed the behemoth-like brick high school, with the corner statue of founder William Woodward, across from the Swifton Shopping Center, at 7001 Reading Road. It was the first free public high school founded west of the Alleghenies.

Every day, 3,600 youngsters, coiffed in crewcuts, dreadlocks, shags, layered and smooth, all landed at what was a tense cross section of the urban microcosm of American society, mid- to late 1960s.

Although I was destined to become a rabbi, my high school years, especially after ninth grade, were centered round the winning tradition of the Woodward Bulldogs football team. After a brief and inglorious stint as a reserve tackle, which landed me with a smashed heel plate and the eternal fear of a 310-pound *teammate* gloomily named Tyrone Maupin, who decided to kick me in the foot after he pounded me onto the field during a scrimmage, I limped into Raleigh Taylor's marching band and the company of the wily Clifton. "Do you know Tyrone?" I asked Clifton, assuming so since they were both black. "Yeah, I know him, fool. That's why I came straight to the band."

No matter: The tooting band, the lean, long-limbed drill team, the airborne cheerleaders, the heroic players—we were all one surge of blue-and-white pompoms, glistening brass, rugged helmets, twirling batons, beating drums, and breathless elation under the Friday-night lights of mid-America's urban grandstand.

We were the Public High School League champions year after year. Not just Tyrone Maupin and Ed Shuttlesworth and the quiet Jewish giant Andy Glas, of gridiron fame. We were the PHSL champs. We could never, ever defeat the Vatican-blessed state champions Moeller and Elder Catholic high schools and were never very enthralled traveling to their vaulted playing fields near sanctuary, rectory, and basins of holy water. But within the more familiar, mainstream Cincinnati city system, we thrived together and maintained a football dominion in that corner of metropolitan America.

The PHSL games were windblown, giddy autumn affairs played under rickety field lights and the supervision of local police. Players, cheerleaders, majorettes, and those of us in the band had to all rush back to the protection of waiting buses and tense drivers after victories at certain less-than-hospitable schools. Rocks were occasionally thrown at us by frustrated Withrow Tigers; some Aiken Falcons splattered our blue-and-white-striped uniforms with eggs.

Some of my former high school chums remember these years with an undeniable residue of racist feelings—they do not remember Woodward or those times very fondly. "All I remember is the hate, the way the blacks kept jumping us, and the fear in the halls," one of my classmates reminisced in a letter sent to me in 2006. On the day after Dr. King was assassinated, April 5, 1968, when the school was shut down by violence and sit-ins, my classmate saw a white female ninth grader in a wheelchair upended and whipped in the hallway by four black boys. Helpless and terrified, unable to stop the beating or contact a school official, he, like many that day, fled home. He's been ashamed and angry ever since, unable to reconcile what he saw with a feeling for racial tolerance.

The young victim recovered from the attack, but was never seen at Woodward again.

I was "jumped" more than once during my six years at Woodward, as was my friend Steve. But I've chosen to gloss over the incidents in my memories of those very full days and nights in and around that student city. It was the 1960s, the decade of "the coming apart," and yet we somehow came together, if unwittingly, daily in that public fortress. We were the thrown-together adolescent coalition of blacks, whites, Jews, gentiles, Midwesterners, Appalachians, disenfranchised, fraternity brats, singers, writers, gymnasts, pimps, and poets who found uneasy common ground in the multicultural clubs and associations of our school.

I remember Eddie Shuttlesworth's huge hands grasping the pigskin (when he wasn't squeezing those trombone valves) as he ran alongside the bulky Andy Glas—who made the all-league squad in our senior year, 1970, and was toasted in more than one local synagogue. Eddie Shuttlesworth, a future draft choice of the Baltimore Colts who wore the crown of 1970 Homecoming King tilted dangerously on his enormous head, also played center on the varsity Bulldogs basketball team (I was the public-address announcer, naturally). When Eddie wasn't carrying the football through a helpless heap of Walnut Hills Eagles, or leaping for an intimidating rebound over a scattering spray of Finneytown Wildcats, his fleshy fingers were constantly in motion, snapping happily—or more often, extending his palm with friendship and warmth. I loved him, Clifton was in awe of him, and Raleigh Taylor mentored him in the brass instruments with a look of affection and hope in his eyes.

The previous fall of 1967, Eddie was injured and marched with the band for three weeks rather than play on the squad. Returning on the bus from a victory at the genteel, suburban Princeton High School, I used him as a shield while making my first sexual advance. Exhaust fumes swirling, wheels rolling extravagantly, the seats noncompliant and maddeningly uneven, I nonetheless found the deliciously zaftig Karen Cummings as irresistible as she was, well, inexperienced. I was in combat with buttons, vests, feathers, belts, her majorette's cap, which she didn't quite understand would be more helpful *off* her head, allowing her abundant strawberry hair to free-fall and dazzle. Something told me, after fifteen minutes of this struggle, and a burst of pre-ejaculation, and Eddie's mountain moving away to service a developing audience, that I was just not making progress on undoing the straps of Karen's elaborate brassiere and landing those victory globes. Finally, we simply kissed, an ecstatic if penultimate rush of lips and breath and foreign aromas that were more exotic than sweet.

It was then that Clifton appeared in the bouncing aisle, jubilant and criminal as he blasted Karen and me with Afro-Sheen hairspray, declaring effervescently, "This is my culture, man!" In that old bus, under cover of friendly shadows, unable to always see colors, we sang, dared, rocked, bellowed; in fact, the only colors that really mattered flew about in Karen Cummings's and her companions' blue and white sparkles.

Meanwhile, the edgy society of Woodward was the product of a communal willingness to explore the national equivalent of Joseph's biblical multicolored coat. It was *real, real, real.* And for those of us from socially progressive homes, whose parents—like my immigrant father—actually knew that the time period of the Civil Rights Movement, Vietnam, the revolt in Czechoslovakia, the transcendent student civil disobedience at Chicago's Democratic Convention when, among other things, a twenty-eight-year-old black state senator named Julian Bond was nominated for the vice presidency of the United States while thousands of kids shouted, "The whole world is watching" outside the convention walls—all of it actually represented an epoch in American and global history.

In 1968, the people's anguish and convictions forced a president to turn down a second term. Lyndon Baines Johnson was a deeply conflicted, foul-mouthed, brilliantly legislative president from Texas who used Southern expletives to describe "*negras.*" But LBJ inspired (or politically arm-locked) the 1964 Civil Rights Act and the 1965 Voting Rights Bill, pulling black Americans out of the nineteenth century. He announced a partial bombing halt in Vietnam on March 31, 1968, as well as his intention not to seek a second term. Johnson had succeeded President John F. Kennedy in Dallas on November 22, 1963—sworn into office within the cramped, sweltering main cabin of Air Force One by a local federal judge, within three hours of Kennedy's murder in Dealey Plaza. Mrs. Kennedy still bore her husband's bloodstains on her immortalized pink dress, next to the unexpected president and within a few feet of her husband's casket. Dignity, grief, disbelief, resentment, constitutional gravity, and the vulnerability of giants hung in that moment and place, as the Boeing 707 lifted off with a new American government and returned to Washington.

When I emotionally crouched in the uncannily small cabin on board that very plane—on display at the Wright Patterson Air Force Base Museum in 1999—I understood that history is the sum of real men and women doing the best or worst they can.

LBJ won a hefty reelection a year later over the archconservative Senator Barry Goldwater and, for a time, became the unlikely ally of Rev. King and the Freedom Movement. He also became a dupe of his generals and his secretary of defense, Robert McNamara, eventually committing hundreds of thousands of drafted youngsters to the tragically misguided and polarizing conflict in Vietnam. The trauma of this war, with its napalm, savagery, corruption, as well as the ravaging of the Vietnamese people and the Indochinese landscape, wove its way into the psyches and lives of Woodward's young men. We were experimenting, as we were supposed to, with sex and cigarettes and alcohol; we were reckless with drugs; we were fantasizing about the girls' hot pants and the way they smelled and felt up close; but we were distracted by the images of body bags and jungle infernos and POWs and the terrifying possibilities that lay in store for us once we graduated high school and student deferments were no longer an escape. We didn't know it then, but the war was being fought by black boys in disproportionate numbers. Flight to Canada, a cold and numb alternative, was being discussed quietly in many white homes—including my own. Twentyish, pale, prelaw advisors came into the school, unofficially, to discuss and explain the details and risks of being a conscientious objector rather than a conscript. I talked to one, while being unable to imagine myself, at seventeen or eighteen, living in an apartment by myself in Winnepeg or Ottawa.

All we boys wanted, however, were car keys and conquests. What we wanted was normal. What we got in '67, '68, and '69 was aberrant but truly indelible. What other generation could decide to pick between Martin Luther King, Jr. ("I have a dream") and Governor George Wallace ("Segregation now, segregation tomorrow, segregation forever!") as role models? What generation since has loved, truly *loved*, a good cross section of our national leaders, be it the grandiloquent Rev. King, or the strangely aloof but perceptive Senator Eugene McCarthy, or the elegiac and compelling and late-maturing Senator Robert F. Kennedy? "Bobby," we called him, who quoted the Greeks, wept with starving black kids in Mississippi, hated the war his brother John had actually begun, and was able to extemporaneously calm a shocked and potentially dangerous crowd of black listeners in Indianapolis on the night that King was murdered in Memphis.

There he was, the imperially slim but magnetic senator, in that moment and place the night of April 4, 1968, bravely announcing the news, and with pastoral brilliance, telling them that he understood the complexity of their anger: "I can only say that I feel in my own heart [this] kind of feeling. I had a member of my family killed, [and] he was killed by a white man." Bobby was murdered at the Ambassador Hotel in Los Angeles by a Palestinian psycho eight weeks later, moments after winning the California Democratic presidential primary and establishing himself as the front-runner for the nomination.

We were afraid, we were wary, we were in danger in those days, but we actually had personal feelings of connection and intimate affinities with many of the men and women who led us in politics, music, poetry, and social justice. We mourned the martyrs of the time, the iconic Kennedy brothers as well as Dr. King. But we also identified with a host of guitarists and lyricists and writers and countless, faceless soldiers, nurses, chaplains, and students, and housewives who marched and even died in favor of a better society that cherished values more than valuables. And the words of the more famous ones—from the Beatles to Bobby—are words that we remember, as clearly as we remember the words of our parents, or the first movie we saw with that certain date, or what transpired in the city high school that I attended from the inception of the federal government's civil rights legislation in 1964 through to Woodstock and the Apollo moon landing of 1969 and, finally, to the bloody coda, just four weeks before our graduation from Woodward—the Kent State massacre of 1970. Four students were killed when Ohio National Guardsmen suddenly opened fire as scores were demonstrating against the war. At the southern end of the state, we Woodward seniors were about to don caps and gowns and take our places in society.

What kept most of us sane and some of us from giving in to the hate?

I truly believe that, from time to time, across six years of secondary school during a decade unique in American history and social cataclysm, a group of youngsters became colorblind. *Being together*—around a Bunsen burner, on the raw tiles of a locker room and shower, in the heaving hallways of a Friday-morning pep rally, at a lunchroom strike protesting lousy food—precipitated some level of tolerance.

If I had matriculated from Yavneh Day School straight into a Hebrew middle school, I would have never met Clifton Fleetwood and—this makes me tremble—perhaps never put a human face in front of the racist notions of black people that prevailed in our white Jewish world of Cincinnati's Roselawn and Amberley Village communities in the 1960s. It didn't matter that a handful of prominent rabbis, some sincere, some publicity-seeking, had been walking with Martin Luther King, Coretta Scott King, Ralph Abernathy, and John Lewis, and that some had also been jailed and beaten in places like Selma, Alabama; Jackson, Mississippi; and Macon, Georgia. We didn't know about these things till later, and if we had not been thrown together with black kids, for good or for ill, would have had no context for them other than the social apartheid that kept them off of our television programs, our cereal boxes, our neighborhoods—even if Ohio did not have state laws on the books that made segregation "legal" and acceptable.

It was hardly easy, and it made some of us more hateful, perhaps, than some white kids who never ate lunch or shared a slide rule with a black classmate and simply remained polite about their racism. There were contemptible people in that high school who were black—bullies, extortionists, gang members who would have made the white elitists blush with their visceral derision of white people and our right to walk a hallway in peace and tranquility. There were some individual black students whom I disliked, for their personalities, their guile, their poor hygiene habits, or their just plain pandering to stereotypes that served their purposes. But I disliked them *personally*, just as I adored Clifton because he was funny and astute and, frankly, didn't regard me as his white friend. Just his friend.

He often philosophized about life, and something he said some forty years ago has remained more succinct and trenchant for me than anything I've read in Talmudic tomes or heard in seminars and treatises about human life. He said, "Attitude, bro. Attitude." That was it. In the two words of his personal aphorism, he summarized everything for me that makes sense and bestows perspective on the predicament of being a person. "Attitude, bro." I have repeated it to myself thousands of times, when under pressure, or angry, or disgusted, or too hasty, or hurt, or triumphant. All the rabbis, church sages, prophets, and psychologists through time have never, in their combined wisdom, offered a pithier motto than Clifton's "Attitude, bro," spoken one afternoon in Room B4 of Woodward High School.

But then King was murdered in Memphis.

After crossing Seymour Road onto the Woodward property on the morning of April 5, Steve and I parted nervously and I began to look for Clifton. There was trouble in the air. I had thought about Clifton through a mostly sleepless night and could not wait to see him—it seemed like the most natural thing, under the circumstances.

But there were no familiar faces to be found as I approached the grounds, now alone. In fact, there would be no school that day, no hall chatter, no band music. A Jewish basketball buddy of mine, Elliott, scurried past me. "Get out of here!" he warned. "I just saw a Negro guy with a crutch swinging it at every white person he can get. I ducked and he just missed me. Goodbye!"

When I arrived at the front circle of the school, directly across Reading Road from the main entrance into Swifton Shopping Center, many of the students were already pouring out of the great front doors. Most of their faces were heated or full of terror. One nasty fellow, his dark face contorted with anger, recognized me: "Kamin, you whitey Jews ought to clear out of here. You all killed Dr. King. We're going to break up the stores across the street." With that, he shoved me so hard that I thought my lungs had collapsed.

Where was Clifton?

It was then that about four hundred black students filed out of the tall entrance doors and walked out onto the front green. They had been engaged in a forlorn sit-in just inside the school since dawn. Now they were still; they had stunned countenances. With great relief, I recognized my friend Clifton.

"Clifton!" I ran toward him as the group milled, and then was stopped by the cold, menacing stares of his compatriots.

Clifton's eyes gave me no encouragement. As he walked past me, he said, in a quivering voice: "No, man. This is not for you."

What ensued was a morning-long, quiet protest and vigil by Clifton and his brothers and sisters. Not one white face was permitted to violate the sea of black pain. From time to time, glass was heard shattering across the street at the shopping center, and sirens wailed.

As city patrol cars began to accumulate around our school, another group of teenagers formed in a far corner of Woodward's front quadrangle. We remained within view of Clifton and the other protestors, but were socially and culturally removed from them and their emotion. The crackle of police walkie-talkies blew in the air between Clifton and me. Even from across this new gulf, I could see and was shaken by the vacuum in Clifton's eyes. As the Cincinnati police, on foot, grim, tentative, spreading through both crowds, ordered us to go home, I thought I saw my country vanishing across the front green of my high school.

The Ville, New Orleans, and Prayer Feathers

t was called "The Ville," and it was hazardous for the white kids. A broad, L-shaped strip of the hallway, it cut a loop not that far down from the main offices of the school. An informal regime of militant, angry, or simply racist black gang leaders and hot-tempered, self-anointed oracles of black power and separation, some of them just petty thieves or ongoing truants, peppered the Ville with danger and discrimination. It was a zone of early African-American self-awareness that did some good in the long run, but was usually an area, in the short run, where white students "got jumped" or at least mocked.

It was large enough to contain the school's only candy machines, though cigarette vending units would have done well. There was an occasional small assembly (and on such mornings or afternoons the Ville was temporarily neutralized) and, indeed, a few ceremonies were held there as it had become, by 1967, the showcase of displays and announcements about prominent black figures, from George Washington Carver to Muhammad Ali to Malcolm X. Gatherings were convened during Black History Month, which generally sincere white assistant principals moderated. The black administrators were rarely heard from at a dais—one wonders now what they really considered in their souls as they roamed the restive crowd with walkie-talkies in hand, at alert. A number of white students derided Black History Month as "a month that never ends" (this is still heard today from white people), and surprisingly few black students paid attention, except for the handful of well-known, high-achieving student poets, dramatists, and philosophers who knew a thing or two about W. E. B. Du Bois and Angela Davis.

The African American experience, with its legacy suffering of white slave-trading, apartheid, and state-sponsored terrorism, had to be expunged and distilled into a new sense of identity and promise for my black classmates at Woodward. Good things were spoken about in the Ville-area hallway meetings mandated by a usually thoughtful school administration that constantly tried to balance the campus's need between patience and police. Glossy posters of Rev. Martin Luther King, Jr., were prominent there and elsewhere, especially after the assassination in Memphis, and the preacher's words hung above us in calligraphy and on banners:

"We must somehow believe that unearned suffering is redemptive."

"Freedom is never voluntarily given by the oppressor; it must be demanded by the oppressed."

But the Ville ultimately became a ghetto of fear and exclusion; most of us "honkies," clutching our algebra and social-studies books, took the steps up to the second floor or down to the basement level in order to bypass its usual denizens, with their shiny, scary smiles, their blaring radios (WHIO Black AM Radio), and their intermittent flashes of burnished blades or threatening chains. I didn't personally know any of the rogues that hung around the

L-shaped province before and after school, but they looked as familiar as they were treacherous. I had no idea then that some of these people were nineteen or even twenty years old, and that not all of them were actually enrolled at our high school.

On April 5, just an hour or so after my cold confrontation with Clifton, as the Cincinnati police swept the school with marked restraint to encourage us to leave, I peeked into the Ville from a peripheral vantage point. It was all but deserted, and I knew that, for my safety, I should exit. I noticed two of those recognizable, hirsute regulars in the far corner—they glared at me from across the L-shaped walkway and I trembled. Suddenly I saw Clifton flash between them, stop for a moment, and talk with them. I did not have the nerve to call out to him, nor did I reasonably think he'd respond. I heard one of them laugh a gurgling cackle, slap Clifton's hand in a kind of fraternal way, and exclaim to my friend(?), "Go on, Fleet!" Then Clifton was gone.

Four black girls entered the far doorway, also heading in tribute, it seemed, towards the two men. None of them appeared to be in mourning for MLK; there was a gloating rhythm, almost a victorious élan, about all of them. Then, from behind me, whistling past, went two husky white boys—a pair of Hartwell-neighborhood types known for their own felonious behavior around the school, as well as their trademark and distinct anti-black sentiments. To my horror, I heard these two seventeen-year olds mutter something out loud about "Martin Luther Coon."

The two hoods, with reckless bravado, driven by the imagery of blood and racial hatred that so permeated our lives in that time and place, put themselves squarely in the middle of the space—challenging the territorial sovereignty of the Ville. I really thought that they were crazy—the two black fellows who stood in dominion across the way were bigger, older, and clearly more experienced. I favored neither side, but was glad that Clifton had come and left, even if my heart ached for a word from him. My thoughts were scattered quickly as the four girls in attendance, as if responding to some cue, rushed at the white boys and attacked with a fury that made my skin crawl.

The girls made quick work of the boys. With surprising alacrity and deftness, their teeth shining in ambush, they paired off and systematically knocked them flat and flailing on the floor. It was hard to tell which of the invaders fared worse: In sync, one girl grabbed a boy from behind while the other rammed a knee upward into his crotch. The boys wailed in pain and cringing humiliation. Both bent over in anguish while the two girls, smaller but chunkier than the boys, though clearly combat-ready, literally punched their lights out with their fists and legs. As the larger and more determined white hood tried to get up and make a comeback, the corresponding heftier girl, groaning in satisfaction and a kind of ancestral comeuppance, fired a right hook directly into his belly, and he collapsed back onto the floor, his nose splattering blood against the foundation. The girls laughed in victory, and their male chiefs mocked the white boys by just watching in contemptuous approval.

I fled the scene, feeling the lifeless eyes from Dr. King's image following me from behind the display glass.

· · · · ·

Running home, a gray midday wind sending intermittent rain drops across my face, I bumped into another one of my black classmates, Reggie Denning. I thought it was curious to discover Reggie at the intersection of Reading Road and Losantiville Avenue—the site of the Roselawn Lutheran Church, which Steve and I passed every morning on our way to the high school. I remember wondering, what was Reggie Denning, a particularly dark-skinned (and accordingly taunted by other blacks) individual, doing at the border of this primarily white/Jewish neighborhood? I know now that this was essentially a racist query, but this was not a day or an era of racial concord. It turned out that Reggie Denning, a solidly built, agile, likable youngster with a wry sense of humor, was just like me on April 5, 1968—scared and going home. We lived but a few blocks from each other, on different sides of Reading Road.

I said: "Reggie, what are you doing?"

"I'm going home, man. All the dudes wanted us to beat up on the white kids and I don't get into that. So they were turning on me. Hey, I may be a coward but I ain't no fool."

He smiled at me, but I did see fear in his eyes. His skin was so black and he appeared deeply troubled, trapped—by the day, by the heated undulation from Memphis, by history, by the burden of his color. In the end, it remains personal, this business of race. I surmised that he had chosen a different route that day than the one chosen by Clifton. But they were both trapped, and always would be on one level or another.

Meanwhile, Reggie and I both craved the same thing on that damp day: Against the harsh winds of assassination and national disintegration, we yearned for a place to alight. We wanted the aprons of our mothers and the prudence of our fathers, the sanctuary of our bedrooms at home, the sounds of cooking and the smells of coffee and sizzling meat, the familiar doorknobs and friendly lamps, the consolation of carefree television programs, and the escape of lazy ball games under the springtime sun. We wanted refuge from murder, fire, war, and politics. He and I parted company, with simpatico gestures and unspoken kinship. It was good for both of us to have crossed paths at that moment.

My heart wasn't beating quite as rapidly now, and I felt a certain relief after crossing Reading onto Losantiville. I was but moments from home and walked slowly. My thoughts drifted to a very hot day near Lake City, Florida, August 1963—the same month in which Rev. King would deliver his enduring "I Have A Dream" oration in Washington, DC.

My father, mother, and my younger brother Sam and I had set out from Cincinnati in my father's prized ivory-white '57 Chevy Impala and taken one of our family trips, this time to Miami Beach. My immigrant dad adored the American countryside and knew of no other travel possibility than of the highways, official state maps, Stuckey's pecan pies, and any good local hamburger place, along with clean, if basic motels that featured well-stocked ice machines and fresh Coca-Colas. My father, a stocky, looming man who was a minor soccer legend and decorated war veteran back in our native Israel, always remained socially progressive. "Kennedy" was a magical name in our household; my father's singular political achievement was being elected as a delegate to the 1972 Democratic Convention on a slate committed to Senator Henry "Scoop" Jackson.

On a smoldering day in August, 1963, we pulled into a filling station, the Chevrolet kicking up bone-dry gravel and dirt into the Florida sky. The Marchers for Jobs and Freedom were preparing to convene in Washington; President John F. Kennedy (who initially opposed the march) had two months left to live. Near Lake City, my father and I stepped out of our car to wash up while an attendant pumped gasoline into the vehicle and wiped the windshield.

In the dust we created, we hadn't noticed a second car that pulled up at the same time. Another father and son, black, were also making their way towards the restrooms. The lad was more or less my age. I wondered which pair of us would get into the toilet first, but it didn't matter. They were headed for the one marked COLORED, off to the right a bit. The door was rotting with grime, the facility had none of the outside glow and finish and sparkle of our WHITE gateway on the left. Shoes crunching on the gravel, the four of us, two worlds, briefly crossed on the path. I noticed that the other father looked down and that his shoulders slumped in his overall straps; the intense sun blocked me from seeing my father's face. But my eyes and those of my counterpart's met directly for a brief instant. I looked into something hollow, anonymous, but strangely defiant. He was not ashamed, or maybe he didn't know to be ashamed, which is what I hoped for in that pubescent intersection of ancient rites and evil laws.

My father and I did our business and he was uncharacteristically silent, which told me everything. When we drove away moments later, I looked into the other family's Rambler station wagon, but again, the western Florida sun blinded me and everything else on the earth.

· · · · ·

Many years later, in the spring of 1974, I saw the Deep South once again. It was a very different mode of transportation, a decidedly independent expedition of college adventure and frolic. At the University of Cincinnati, I sang with the Men's Glee Club, which (recalling Woodward) was a rainbow of tenors, baritones, basses, gays, straights, blacks, whites, and Asians—with a sometimes revealing disparity in voice skills and harmonic standards. We had the wound-up choral princes, the slap-happy jazz pianists, the pedantic sheet-music purveyors, the foot-tappers who were personable, the prima donnas who were not. Some of us read music, some of us read porno, many of us were read the riot act by our director, the youthful but intense Bill Ermey. But I liked the proximity to the men of diverse circumstances, the "in-your-face" gestalt of the bus rides to local church recitals, and the campus concerts at the women's dormitories, where there was both fanfare and friskiness.

The bass, Larry Tidrow, an energetic three-hundred-pound linebacker from MLK High School in Louisville who wanted to become a preacher, was caught in a tryst with the sleek and chalky-white seductress Beth Close—who was not a member, but rather a Men's Glee Club groupie. They were well into groping and necking by the back pond of Memorial Hall—the smallest and most secluded of the women's residences, directly across from the College-Conservatory of Music. I respected Larry's magnetic personality and his knowledge of black history, but I never cared for his slightly overbearing ways—particularly in light of the fact that Beth Close was a Woodward alumna, class of '71, upon whom I had an unrelenting crush at the school, and whose fragrant lips once melted into mine just outside Band Room B4. Now I understood that Beth, a crystal-eyed preacher's daughter herself, had a yen for ethnic types—a Japanese weaver and an Egyptian poet had followed me and preceded the irrepressible Larry Tidrow.

It was the first time since graduating from Woodward in 1970 that I again felt the nourishing American mosaic of cultures and habits—and, only months before entering rabbinical school, the nascent sense that my Judaism, though the river of my soul, is not the only water that cools me. We parented Christianity, there's God in everyone, and, as the Bible says, "All rivers run to the sea."

So the gospel music we performed sang to me; the compositions by Lionel Hampton lifted me; the Chinese bamboo melodies fascinated me. But it was the predominant swirl of white boys and black boys, some actual musicians, others (like me) fledgling historians, engineers, pharmacists, attorneys, athletes—this was the rhythm and the beat that made me cleave to the upstart "UC" Men's Glee Club.

Our repertoire ranged from Patrick Gilmore's Dixie-heritage "When Johnny Comes Marching Home," to Schubert's martial, Prussian "Geist der Liebe." In a way, I was back in the band, looking for Clifton, who was already lost to me four years, but black boys were jiving and white boys were whistling and music was happening and colors weren't mattering and my spirit was soaring.

Ultimately, we performed mostly classic vocals and many freedom songs inspired by the still fresh memory of Dr. King. The preacher was gone six years when the club crossed the Mason Dixon line from Cincinnati for a grand tour of the South. We planned logistics, raised money, and studied tunes for several months in preparation for this milestone journey. Richard M. Nixon was losing his presidency, *The Brady Bunch* was concluding its five-year television run, and Hank Aaron, the quiet black slugger for the Atlanta Braves, was toppling Babe Ruth as the all-time home-run king of baseball. But we fifty Glee Club men were thinking about Bourbon Street and the "hurricanes" being served up at Pat O'Brien's.

Indeed, our destination was New Orleans; in between lay a series of performances in auditoriums and church halls from Kentucky to Mississippi. We'd be spending our last night of the two-week odyssey in Memphis, which intrigued me, of course. It was 1974, but—as we singers, narrators, instrumentalists, and one female soloist (a happy, buxom contralto named Bunny Firestone, who was never lonely at the back of the bus) were soon to learn—it might as well have been 1934 in such towns as Welch, West Virginia, and Veramayne, Tennessee.

Arriving one afternoon in the latter community, we were greeted by the local church leaders. It was in their house of worship that we would perform our nightly repertoire of show tunes, ballads, and folk songs. Our conductor was always first off the bus. Bill Ermey, thin as a reed, endowed with an iron will that kept our libidos at bay even as our voices were in sync, would make the preliminary arrangements as to setup, equipment checks, and housing.

In this Tennessee borough, however, Bill ran into a little bit of a problem. The town fathers and mothers had peered into the windows of our charter bus and, alas, noticed a healthy sprinkling of black faces among us fifty young men. They gathered into a tight circle of discussion and duplicity as we boys looked out the window. Two or three of them pulled Bill aside, away from the bus, and spoke to him. There would apparently be no houses available for the "Negro boys" to lodge in.

I remember Bill's face as he dragged himself up the steps of the bus. The late afternoon sun emphasized his paleness and pain. "They won't let us all sleep in their homes," he spoke in agony over the static-filled microphone. "Our black members are supposed to spend the night in the motel down the road."

"And they expect us to think of their church as a house of God," called out Larry Tidrow from the rear, already contemplating his career as a Baptist pastor. *They ought to have seen you and Beth Close by the pond,* I thought to myself, ruefully. But his sentiment was being echoed in the throats and hearts of every one of us who sat, stunned, in a Greyhound bus that was now the vehicle of a new and dreadful awareness.

"Well, boys," said Bill now, his voice suddenly strong and thrilled, "I'm your leader. And I say that if we can't all sleep in their houses, then none of us can sing in their church." In the dim light, I saw that Bill's normally pasty face shone with something I had not seen before. He would be among the first people I personally knew that died of AIDS as the still rowdy '70s spilled into the insensible '80s, but no one had better blood at that moment in Tennessee.

"Well, that's M-L-K with me!" chimed in the uncontainable Reverend Tidrow.

A burst of cheering and applause rocked the bus, along with a booming cadence of "It's M-L-K with me!" Bill turned his narrow back around in the doorway, leaned out, and yelled to the nearby cluster of church leaders:

"We're sorry, people, but we will not be singing here tonight. But we do propose that you have a meeting tonight in your church and ask God why these nice boys lost their voices while passing through this town of yours."

The University of Cincinnati Men's Glee Club wound up sleeping aboard the Greyhound that night, parked alongside US 231 in a rather dreary roadside stop that sucked in the darkness. We, however, laughed and sang and eventually slept as cheerfully as our teacher's convictions had been inspired back down the road at a church with no god.

It was about 3:00 in the morning when I slipped out of the bus, past snoring bodies and a few members who read quietly with flashlights or just rested. Several others had also chosen to step or sleep outside. It turned out to be a crisp night, scented with magnolias and crowned with moonlight.

There had been the necessary bravura following the ugliness at Veramayne, and it was easy to feel proud and cleansed by our decision to depart the scene and, of course, to not sing in that community church. I was very satisfied with that. But I struggled with why it even had to happen, and I remembered Clifton's face on the morning after Dr. King was gunned down, and I recalled Reggie Denning's trembling presence later that day when we encountered each other, both fleeing home from our school—our temple of education, our *community.*

What is it to be black? I wondered. How could anyone who isn't black even imagine the yoke of it, the pounding griefs, the relentless degradations, the legacy of slavery and chains and lynchings and unspeakable shackled ocean passages, the mothers and sisters with bowed heads submitting to the avarice of drunken and psychotic white men who measured their sexuality by a sick dominion over African women who had no empowerment, no space on the same continent as the greatest experiment in democracy ever attempted on this planet?

Who could know what Clifton felt, why he really pulled away? Who else but another black man could understand Martin Luther King's obsessive appetite for food, cigarettes, and women, even as he taught the Gospel—unless you are willing to imagine the feeling, every waking moment, of expecting imminent beatings and being jailed repeatedly just because you're asking for what God intended in a civilization? Who could possibly conceive of what Dr. King reportedly knew unequivocally—that he would be murdered exactly as it happened at the Lorraine Motel on April 4, 1968? To live with that, to *know that*, is a burden simply inconceivable to the vast majority of white men in America, and something of it, real or perceived, still clings to the collective consciousness of American black men. It doesn't matter if you're a renowned baseball player with genuine philanthropic achievements, a surgeon, a newspaper editor, or a preacher in the decades since Woodward High School and MLK: a black man in every one of these categories has personally told me that he has noticed white women pull their purses closer in as he passed by in a mall, or noticed that white families clustered together or pushed their car's power locks as he walked harmlessly by, thinking about his own kids or how the stock market would affect his portfolio.

I looked up at the starry Tennessee sky that night in the spring of 1974. What is it about human nature that some people need to make others smaller? I thought. The Germans and what they did to the Jews. The Americans and what we did to the Native tribal nations of this New World, even as white Americans wound up killing each other mercilessly between 1861 and 1865 in a Civil War that took more American lives than any other conflict, including World War II. The British and their domination and slaughter of Indians; the incomprehensible caste system of India itself. The Japanese and their butchery of the Chinese; the Turks and their genocide of Armenians; the staggering carnage in the Balkans, Indochina, myriad African wars and famines, the blood of Jerusalem.

I got up and spoke at that little parallel sit-in demonstration at my high school on April 5, 1968, because Martin Luther King—a flawed, brilliant, frightened, and brave man—inspired me to think of religion as social justice. Here was a visible paragon of a minister translating scriptural ethics into action, turning the text into life. So many of his own colleagues tried to upend him; they were jealous, small-minded, apprehensive, afraid of change, or too radical for his doctrine of nonviolence. When he stood at the Riverside Church in New York on April 4, 1967—exactly one year before Memphis—and spoke out against the Vietnam War, almost every prominent black American, including one U.S. senator, upbraided and rebuked him for mixing the war issue with civil rights—as if the two weren't irrevocably intertwined on every level. The preacher was unable not "to bring the war into the field of my moral vision"—was everyone else really that blind for that long? President Lyndon Johnson broke with King over this, feeling personally betrayed that the reverend asked a question about a war that was killing thousands weekly while bread and books were denied to poor Americans of every color.

I realized, staring up at the sky that night in Tennessee, why I was going to rabbinical school. Somebody in my country had put the Bible into action, and had been scorned, smitten, and stoned just like Amos, Isaiah, Ezekiel, and Jeremiah—who generally fared no better for their moral visions.

How could church men and women in 1974, after the civil rights revolution of the '60s, after the Voting Rights Act of 1965, after Vietnam, after the Holocaust, look into a busload of singing college students and say that anybody was not welcome in their house? It occurred to me that night that I could never accept such a proposition—no matter what the source of such skewed righteousness. I've seen Christians do it, I've certainly seen Jews do it, and my adult daughters surely have observed that Muslims can do it. King, ignited by Gandhi, really wasn't preaching exclusively for African Americans. He was trying to save God for all of us because he obviously knew that God dwells in a spiritually vindicated Greyhound bus or in a troubled high school as surely as God dwells in the corporate-style headquarters of so many national institutions of organized religion.

I climbed back into the bus, through which the fresh night air mercifully flowed via open windows. Larry Tidrow smiled at me and I playfully punched his titanic right shoulder, though it gave me a certain greedy pleasure. I made something of a sleeping space in my seat, closed my eyes, and dreamed of Hopi Indians: A small group of Hopi holy men tied prayer feathers to the feet and hands of Martin Luther King. They gently covered his lifeless face with a cloud-like flower of raw cotton that symbolizes the one heaven. I saw myself completing the ritual by placing a stick in the preacher's grave, so that there would be a ladder for his spirit to climb and return to his ancestors—far, far away from Birmingham, Selma, Chicago, and Veramayne, Tennessee.

· · · · ·

After three days and two rowdy nights in New Orleans—the long-ago pre-Katrina New Orleans—that was deliciously wicked and crowded with nonstop revelers, unhinged alcoholics, nauseatingly exotic whores, and virulent pickpockets, we cleaned out our digestive passages, rubbed our eyes, downed aspirins, and wondered how good it really had been. Larry Tidrow was arrested when a prostitute's trick—and the girl—turned on him. All of us contributed to his bail, and Bill Ermey (who avoided all the nighttime carousing and put us "in your own trust") acted like he didn't know about it. I did notice the conductor, his eyes shut in appreciation and awe, sitting serenely late one afternoon at Preservation Hall, taking in the rolling, improvised jazz blues of ancient black men who turned the heavy air into poignant sound with their saxophones, clarinets, bass guitars, and drums. I imagined Raleigh Taylor sitting there, a more muscular, dark-haired version of the slight, sad conductor who drew some healing from what were pure strains made by men who knew the prevailing sadness of Southern life.

From New Orleans, sobered-up, chastened, not as oblivious to the Greyhound bus fumes as we had been earlier, we headed to the Keesler Air Force Base at Biloxi, Mississippi. The bus traveled on the same highway upon which the starlet Jayne Mansfield had, in 1967, been killed in a horrific car accident. Singing for the blue-clothed airmen and women in a gray hangar, we realized that America was remarkable, as it contained both the brothels of New Orleans and the barracks of Biloxi at two ends of the same causeway along the Gulf Coast.

We arrived in Memphis just before the evening concert scheduled at a local university. The performance was rushed, the sound system tentative, and Bunny, our female soloist, having not recovered from her own exploits in New Orleans, left the tour, exhausted and quite ill. A taxi took her unceremoniously to the airport; Larry Tidrow looked depressed about it and sang a number of wrong lyrics that night in Memphis. There was no opportunity to visit the Mason

Temple, where Dr. King had given his hauntingly prophetic "Mountaintop" speech the night before his murder. I vowed to return to Memphis in the future.

We were all preoccupied with returning home to Cincinnati the next day, and there would be an early start. The grand tour of Southern churches, New Orleans haunts, and plantation back roads had deepened our awareness of our country's chronicles as well as its wounds. We had slept in the bus in social protest and had performed a cantata on board a Mississippi River steamboat. We had shared each other's food and rituals. We roomed together in motels that were once strictly segregated. We added the sins of Veramayne to the fields of our moral visions.

· · · · ·

In June 2006, a few days after returning again from Memphis and New Orleans, I placed a call to the "information" operator in Cincinnati. I had learned earlier that a Clifton Fleetwood was living at the same address listed for him in our Woodward graduation yearbook of 1970. I offered the name and the street and requested the phone number. Two letters to Clifton, written in my own handwriting and asking him to contact me, had gone unanswered but were not returned. I held my breath on the phone line. The operator courteously announced:

"Clifton is here, but the number is unpublished."

3

Room 306

Ever since leaving Woodward High School, I have maintained a furtive relationship with a once-unknown and crumbling motel on Mulberry Street in central Memphis. The Lorraine Motel, one of the only places where black people could even stay in the city, nondescript, unattractive, and a foreclosed property in 1982, is a place about which I have actually dreamed—I've wanted desperately to tell Dr. King not to step out of his favored room, 306, just before 6:00 P.M. on Thursday, April 4, 1968. In my dream, MLK is putting out another cigarette into the plain ashtray and he can't hear me.

The preacher both gathered information and clowned around in an auxiliary room, 201, just two hours earlier—this I also see in my dream. The pillows and linens in the room remain strewn about because, in a burst of uncharacteristic glee, he's just thrown his special aide Andrew Young across one of the two beds and a pillow fight—as if among boys in need of a frolic—has ensued with Young, best friend Rev. Ralph Abernathy, younger brother A. D. King, and others. Dr. King is bellowing and childish and hungry for dinner at Rev. Billy Kyles's new home, and he cannot hear me warning him about the viper across the way in Bessie Brewer's boardinghouse. He can hear Young telling Dr. King that, after a full day in court, an injunction against their proposed next march with Memphis's striking garbage workers has been partially stayed, and he can hear Dr. King teasing Young about not letting him know all day. "You've got to tell the leader, Andy," he taunts.

Soon enough, he returns to Room 306 to shave, using a muddy depilatory formula of water and Magic Shave Powder. He has sensitive skin, can't use a razor, and has no alternative but to resort to the malodorous mixture, which Ralph Abernathy tries to dispel in 306 by splashing on extra cologne. Billy Kyles arrives, and he, King, and Abernathy talk about revivals and travel schedules and soul food, while King changes into a clean white shirt with a wider collar for his thickening neck (which will be blown apart imminently, along with his jaw). They also share relief that Andy Young finally came back with better news from the Shelby County courthouse that afternoon, after being unable to communicate with King all day.

Many African Americans today have cellular phones like everybody else, but King and his peers sometimes were not even permitted to use public telephones. In Room 306, just before 6:00 P.M., King is loud and vibrant; but for me, through hindsight about the assassin across the way in his bathroom lookout, there is silence.

Of course, the drab motel of my historical fantasies does really exist, as does the resilient river city that brings Tennessee, Arkansas, and Mississippi together at a bittersweet juncture of water, blood, geography, and history. So I decided to go see the motel for myself, in June 2006, and to listen to those who were there then, and some who were not.

Flying in through purple mists and hovering ghosts, the plane reeling from the clouds and rain, I feel MLK's sad spirit floating over the grayish Mississippi River, the green landscape, and the brownish buildings below. Ball fields, freeways, and strip malls identify the city as boilerplate American. Yet something languorous rises, like a reluctant steam, betraying this as a painfully unique Southern city. Its black soil is overgrown with forced transition, clinging melancholy, and a shining, reigning FedEx hub where cotton and genteelism once ruled. The cellular twenty-first century has arrived in Memphis, but the communal twentieth century lingers.

Clifton, you should be here with me, I said to myself, remembering the morning of April 5, 1968, as I walked through the drab, conventional-looking Memphis International Airport, feeling much closer to my native, muggy Cincinnati than to sleek and dry Southern California, where I now live. The airport retained a bricklike 1960s ambiance, with none of the hustle and bustle of Cincinnati's glistening and tram-driven Delta hub, or the air-megalopolis, multi-terminaled space center that I had just transferred from in Houston. There was a skinny, wizened shoe-shine guy, several new concessions designed to be "Memphis-centric." But the overall effect remained stolid and vaguely comforting. The standard post-9/11 security channels processed the relatively small crowds with practiced ease. I looked around, en route to the Hertz courtesy shuttle, wondering which passageway or tunnel accepted the R. S. Lewis & Sons Funeral Home casket of the martyred MLK while Clifton Fleetwood and I were separating on the Woodward green. For me, there are shadows in the daytime just as there are dreams in the night.

"Good afternoon, ladies and gentleman, my name is Eleesha, and I will be with you for the next five to seven minutes as we make our way from the terminal to the Hertz rental center." Eleesha was cheerful, corpulent, energetic in her yellow-accented gray Cintas "outside" uniform that vaguely recalled an Explorer Scout getup. She was maybe twenty-five years old—neither of her parents, wherever they were, would have nimbly handled the oversized, air-conditioned, monitor-laden business van back in 1968, when Martin Luther King made three fateful trips to Memphis and was picked up at the airport by private cars from the black community.

Belinda at the rental-car counter was also black—though older than Eleesha—thick, upbeat, responding warmly to my expressions of delight at being there in the chilled rental center rather than the sticky Memphis afternoon outside, as well as my inclusions of "ma'am" and "thank you" at every opportunity. But there was something, I conceded to myself, something solicitous about the way we white liberals treat black folks, perhaps especially in Memphis or Atlanta or Birmingham, although we truly lack a desire to patronize them. We're sorry about something, or everything, and we don't really know how to be ourselves around them, though we genuinely wish to be.

Belinda reacted to my request for directions to the Marriott Memphis Downtown with a map and then meticulously wrote out directions with a dry marker, from the very Hertz exit gate to the entranceway circle of the hotel. She was very eager to help and explain. "What brings you to Memphis?"

"I'm writing a book about Dr. King, and a high school friend I sort of lost on the morning after King was killed. I'm going to the Lorraine Motel—my first visit there."

Belinda was pleased and there was generosity in her eyes. "Well, the Lorraine is very close to your hotel. The trolley can take you there very easily."

It took several moments for the air-conditioning unit in my Ford Focus to actually cool things down as I headed along Interstate 240 West/North to Union Avenue in the downtown area. The outside temperature was 95 degrees. Memphis seems to *want* to be seen, even as stubborn old neighborhoods give way to postmodern structures and corporate centers. Journalist Gerold Frank wrote, not long after MLK was killed: "Memphis is staid and prosaic, far more like a Dutch town than the Egyptian capital of antiquity for which it is named. It breathes the languid air of the old South, an air of many generations of respectability and propriety, of son succeeding father and grandson succeeding son as planter, farmer, merchant, lawyer, white-collar worker."

There are traces of all this along the fringes of Memphis's environment, but America has long lost its distinctive regions. Birmingham was long ago dubbed "Pittsburgh of the South," and Florida, save for its panhandle and the Tallahassee region, is a colony of Disney with a mix of Jewish cold cuts, while Memphis is the corporate locus of Federal Express, Graceland, and an array of fiery, competing barbecue-sauce ventures.

Memphis has survived the post–Civil War Irish-black backlash violence, and the yellow-fever epidemics of the nineteenth century, and the murder of the American moral leader of the twentieth century. But when I ventured off Belinda's prescribed route to the Marriott, dodged the trolley marked "Civil Rights Museum" on the track-laden thoroughfare, and diverted to Main at Mulberry Street, time stopped. Woodward High School froze, my parents wiped their tears, Clifton brushed past me, Mr. Taylor shut his eyes in pain, and my inner life welled up from under the deeply gray sky of that June afternoon.

The sign! The balcony! My eyes were familiar with the images from a thousand reproductions on television, movies, and in newsprint, but the real sight almost blinded me. But it wasn't from light—the day was pale and doleful, and the clouds covered the earth and the few grieving dogwoods and the railings and the blue doors and the drawn white curtains across the expanse of the immortal motel. No, it wasn't from light that I was blinded, but from the almost incomprehensible sense that the Lorraine was real, the balcony setback where the father of my soul, freshly shaven, hungry for dinner, lay dying was actually in my line of vision, and that the debilitating and life-altering events at my high school the morning after the Lorraine murder were truly connected to something now, more than ever, dreadfully factual.

Yes, this is for me, Clifton.

It wasn't a dream this time.

I looked to my left at the extension of the National Civil Rights Museum (which encompasses the Lorraine Motel)—in what was Mrs. Brewer's two-story boardinghouse in 1968. Flinching, I noticed the infamous bathroom window of the restored, now archival structure that had been the sniper's nest on April 4. I heard the sharp report inside my head, saw the trajectory of the .30–06 rifle bullet across the gulley of weeds and bushes, traversing the slope into the corner of the balcony where Dr. King stood and spoke to Rev. Jesse Jackson and others below about a certain hymn he hoped to hear that evening.

There were few people about, that gray and darkening damp afternoon when I first beheld the most important coordinates of my educational and spiritual life, there on Mulberry Street in Memphis. From my rented car, I observed the wreath that sits outside Room 306, and the two white limousine Cadillacs that remain parked beneath the railings forever. The gunfire was gone, the passersby unafraid, the boardinghouse harmless, the museum façade literally growing out of the standing wing of the motel and taking it in like a mother sustaining a wounded child.

I stared at the dashboard of my indifferent Ford Focus and broke down, a muffled cry bursting out of my throat as primal as the blood was up on the balcony.

Two hours later, I boarded the "Riverfront Loop" trolley, a pale light finally emerging in the twilight hours of the extended June evening. Placing the required, exact-change, single-dollar bill into the fare box (it really is an honor system), I sat myself directly across from a mother and her two little girls.

The Memphis trolley system, operated by the Memphis Area Transit Authority (MATA), uses historically authentic cars acquired from Portugal, Australia, Brazil, and New Orleans. The 2.5-mile long, $33 million double-track route, laid down over the literal ruins of the central city and the ashes of the former streetcars that vanished in 1947, began operating twenty-five years after the MLK murder, in 1993. My seat, wooden, cozy, ventilated by a forgiving breeze from the open windows, was wide enough for two—and the younger girl across from me almost immediately eyed the space on my bench.

"You can sit here," I smiled at the child, her hair perfectly arranged in a high bun and adorned with a bright blue ribbon. Her face was smooth, pure ebony; her eyes were two seas of vanilla innocence.

She jumped over, allowing more room for her pleasant and approving young mother and her sister to enjoy their adjacent perch. I am so struck by the recollection of that beautiful child, Tiera, who chatted amiably with me as the car turned toward the river and crossed the Illinois Central Railroad River Line bed, grinding its way affably past the Pyramid arena and convention center, the Mud Island Monorail connection, and a host of trendy eateries, loft developments, and gallerias. Tiera looked squarely into my face and she *did not* see color, or the reflection of it in my eyes. She smiled back at her sister, Victoria, and her mother, Vicky—thirtyish, lovely, so smart, unafraid, as they cavorted on the trolley while enjoying a day of middle-class shopping and exploring in central Memphis that MLK could never have even imagined.

The conductor, a diminutive, energetic white fellow who also took on the aura of a genial master of ceremonies, called out each stop with gusto and pride. "Spaghetti Warehouse! Anybody feel like spaghetti?" The sparse but relaxed and integrated crowd on the trolley enjoyed his frivolity. He walked over to Vicky, however, and said, quietly, "Actually, ma'am, you and your girls have already gone around once on the loop, but it's okay, I won't charge you again." He winked at me, meaning well, I thought, but I didn't find the gesture appealing. Perhaps it was racially patronizing. But I thought I heard something repentant in his eagerness to let Vicky know that she would now be his guest. Perhaps there was some rueful Southern language in the exchange that I will think about for a long time.

Meanwhile, it's doubtful that Tiera, who described every dimension of her recent seventh birthday party to me, will ever really understand what Dr. King's blood, spilled within a constant short radius of the "loop," had to do with her carefree spending spree that afternoon and her unguarded discourse with a white man writing a book.

The trolley turned southbound, after traversing some warehouse areas that were tidier than they had once been, and clanged mirthfully onto Main Street. Past, present, and future passed by through the open air of the New South as dusk eased in and the lights of downtown sparkled. An evening crowd of couples and families, truly integrated and tranquil, walked among the fountains and office towers of the Civic Center. Vicky, Victoria, and Tiera hopped off, bidding me a fond goodbye and best wishes, as the mother's cell phone lit up and I realized that it was really getting dark. I wanted to stroll with them, but heard Clifton's voice in my ear: "This is not for you, man."

· · · · ·

For my part, I could not disembark from the pleasant tram. As it circled again (the conductor also appeared to "let me slide," as we used to say back at Woodward High School) and re-approached the riverbanks, darkness set in, though the trolley and the community were well lit. All the other passengers had left but for Robert F. Kennedy, who sat where Vicky had just sat, and smiled at me with his broad, youthful teeth, and his bushy hair tossing in the breeze.

"I saw little girls and boys like that child, but they weren't so lucky. It was 1968, and you were in high school and I was running for president. But that's not why I was there to visit those starving kids, in the fullest sense."

"I remember, Senator. You were in Mississippi, maybe not that far from here." I also recalled to myself that Bobby Kennedy was brought back from New York to Arlington National Cemetery in Virginia for burial, and that it was also aboard a train. The railway cortège ran late because so many people poured out along the tracks to wave goodbye—in fact, two spectators were accidentally killed by the train near Elizabeth, New Jersey. Two months earlier, Lorene Bailey, the telephone receptionist at the Lorraine Motel, had died, in panic, of a cerebral hemorrhage after the shot downed Martin Luther King. These are things that I remember, just as I remember the Woodward motto, *Esse quam videri*—"To be, rather than to seem."

I continued the conversation: "I went to sleep in my room on Bluefield Place in Cincinnati, Senator, late at night on June 5 of '68. I knew you had been shot and I cried into my pillow till the wee hours. One of your Ohio campaign workers, an idealistic man about twenty-two, had just stayed with us a couple of weeks before. He had worked at the same summer camp with me in Indiana. I remember—he was also a Bobby, though his last name was Rosenfield. I just thought he was the greatest—it was almost like he *was* you. He and I talked and talked about the loss of Dr. King and how you had become the last hope for the minorities, for all the people who felt cut off from everything because of Vietnam, because the Republicans were going to nominate Nixon, but most of all because Dr. King had been cut down. Really, you were the one that people looked to. After all those years of people seeing you as a kind of arrogant, antagonistic lawyer trying to protect your family's interests and root out mob types, the guy who only jumped into the presidential race once Eugene McCarthy cleared the way with his own run against Vietnam, you became, in '68, the poet and the hope for little people. My black friends who still talked to me at high school after MLK would say, 'Well, maybe at least we've got Bobby.' It seemed like the terrible grief of your brother's assassination gave you some kind of bittersweet perception, and even teenagers like me, well, nerds who watched Huntley-Brinkley and read *Life* magazine and really lamented things, and dreaded the rioting and chaos in our streets, sensed that you had grown. You were telling us that there really was suffering out there, in the ghettos and on the farms. Anyway, I fell asleep that awful night about four A.M., and then awoke, as I did every day, at seven, and flipped on the hourly NBC Radio News on WLW Radio. I heard your press secretary, Ron Nessen, announce that you had not survived the bullet wound to your head. You need to know—and this place seems to be so apropos to my finally saying this to you, that my friends and I cried like children who had just buried their father a few weeks earlier and now had to bury their stepfather. We hurt, not like your own family, of course, but we were damaged and frightened and I can feel that now. It's a part of me and a lot of other people about my age. We had something mercurial in you and King and now we were orphaned. I will never forget your younger brother, Ted, saying in his cracking voice, so tortured, at your funeral service in New York, 'Love is not an easy feeling to put into words.'"

Who lived in 1968, with any consciousness, who does not know that America was once a family that mourned, and had things worth consecrating?

I was having a conversation, and weeping openly, with Senator Robert Francis Kennedy on board the Riverfront Loop trolley in Memphis, Tennessee, thirty-eight years after the national trauma of my collective adolescence.

He remained focused on one thing.

"I never saw such poverty and hunger and malady as I did that spring," said RFK. The trolley ran along the river in dark stillness. "I don't know that I ever really thought about those kinds of things until after my brother was killed. My God, what you kids saw in those years." He sighed, a thin veil of compassion and insight falling across his face. "I came out of the shell of my upbringing. My brother was killed and I realized some things were more important than others. The hunger and privation of those kids and their families in those shacks in our own country were rancid and humiliating to our nation. What you and your classmates saw—that's why you're here, aren't you? The war that made no sense and that was eating your generation; the two cultures in our country, black and white, so hateful and violent towards one another; and what happened to King, to my brother, and to me." He turned his head and I saw the hole in his skull from the Ambassador Hotel in Los Angeles, June 5, 1968.

"But you learned a lot about yourself, didn't you, Senator, before you died?"

And then the trolley veered onto Main Street, and the blues could be heard in the distance, and there was the delicious smell of sizzling barbecue sauce, and the Lorraine Motel quickly fell into view, one block over to the right on Mulberry. RFK was gone, and I shut my eyes and opened them just in time to see Dr. King falling backwards off the train, and there was Billy Kyles running over with the orange bedspread from Room 306 to cover Martin and keep him warm. I leaned out and twisted my neck as far as I could to see what was happening—even though I knew—but all I could see now was the shrubbery and a red light flashing somewhere, and I knew that the motel was real and that I would never quite wake up from being fifteen years old in America in 1968.

In the morning I would go back to the Lorraine Motel and the National Civil Rights Museum. But now, I fled from the trolley when it stopped at the Marriott, my heart pumping with both terror and validation. In Memphis that night, I slept fitfully, the sounds of mortar and young men screaming in pain ringing in my ears, and the sight of proud garbage men carrying placards declaring "I AM A MAN" flickering across my closed eyes. Dr. King, this is for me, isn't it?

4.

Memphis Voices

lack men, not servile, but focused and hard-working, attended to me in the morning after my arrival in Memphis. Following a gruesome night in my hotel bed, fighting pillows and ghouls, the dawn came through, bright and restorative.

Downstairs, twenty-one-year-old Rodney, chunky and talkative, who worked both the "Trolley Stop" bar and the "Magnolia Grille" restaurant, refreshed my coffee cup. "Did you see that game last night, Mister? Miami gonna whip Detroit tonight too!" He was referring to the semifinal championship NBA basketball game between the Detroit Pistons and the Miami Heat. "Man, the Shaq, he was all over Richard Hamilton. The Shaq, he everything." Rodney, who calls himself "The Analyst," was raving about Miami's renowned Shaquille O'Neal, truly one of the finest athletes in the world and much more of an icon to young black men today than, say, any given living civil rights leader.

"But nobody was ever better than Michael Jordan," I offered.

"Michael the greatest," said the Analyst. "But he ain't nothing without Scottie." Rodney was right—Michael Jordan, a legend, would not have been the stratospheric success that he was with the invincible Chicago Bulls of the 1990s without the constant aerodynamic assistance of forward Scott Pippen.

"Well, you're too young to have seen some of the guys I saw, Rodney. I saw the Big O and Wilt the Stilt," referring to Oscar Robertson of my hometown (and now extinct) Cincinnati Royals and the incomparable Wilt Chamberlain of the San Francisco (now Golden State) Warriors, who once scored 100 points in a single game, and was also famed for having scored with literally thousands of women.

"The Big O was awesome, no question. But he had his best years with Milwaukee." Rodney was also correct there. He proceeded to unfurl a verbal scoreboard of facts and opinions about the National Football League, boxing, and major league baseball. His focus was on personalities: Hoopster LeBron James of the Cleveland Cavaliers, boxer James "Lights Out" Toney, Yankees shortstop Derek Jeter, Pittsburgh Steelers running back Jerome "The Bus" Bettis, and again and again, "Shaq."

Clifton and I used to have these kinds of discussions in the Woodward hallways, and he, too, preferred the African American basketball legends to those of the other sports. By the time the Cincinnati Reds of professional baseball, my team and my sport, became the historic "Big Red Machine" in 1970, we had completed high school and Clifton had vanished from everything but my memory.

"What about MLK, Rodney?"

"I read all about MLK. Come back and talk to me tonight." I made sure that I would.

At the front door of the hotel, two valets—young, heavyset Bobby, and an ancient but vital, sinewy man named Elmo—greeted me and had my car retrieved. I asked Elmo if he was there in Memphis in 1968. "Oh, yes I was, sir. Remember it well." We also agreed to talk that night, after he finished his shift.

The sun, a reluctant ball, had broken through the gray cloud cover, and downtown was at a midmorning business bustle. At the Peabody Hotel, a Memphis landmark where the ambitious meet and the ducks take their famed red-carpet walk to and from the Grand Lobby twice daily, to the tune of John Philip Sousa's "King Cotton March," I sat down with Micah Greenstein, the young senior rabbi of Memphis's flagship Temple Israel.

"The trees are beautiful here," Micah told me about Memphis. He was polished, immaculately shaven, fit, with a runner's physique that was reined in by his quiet, pin-striped rabbinic suit. On appearance, he did not seem the type to claim an affinity with the black liturgies and the Baptist hymns. He didn't look like somebody who would have walked leisurely through the halls of Woodward High School. But Micah's father served as rabbi at another Temple Israel—in Dayton, just fifty miles from Cincinnati, in 1968. "It was a turbulent time," he told me, and I smiled deferentially, not particularly requiring this well-intentioned young man to tell me that it was a turbulent time. He said, "I remember a few riots at the high school next door to the Jewish day school I attended."

I realized that there were many Woodwards on the morning of April 5, 1968—how many Cliftons walked away from white boys like me? In fact, there were disturbances all across Ohio that morning, from Woodward in Cincinnati, to Colonel White High School in Dayton, to Eastmoor in Columbus, to Cleveland Heights High. Micah Greenstein spoke about being the only white child in his Cub Scout troop. "My parents were pleasantly surprised when they attended the year-end dinner for the troop."

I beheld this strapping rabbi with his curly hair and chiseled face—a paragon of the postmodern rabbinate, with cellular and Blackberry attachments and a full, corporate-style operation waiting for him at the regal Temple Israel, an 1,800-family megacenter of Southern Jewish life, programming, and endowment strategies standing on stately, shady East Massey Road. The congregation observed its 150th anniversary in 2004, and there are many historical documents in its various collections of the temple's involvement in American history. The Web site notes: "When our country entered into World War I in 1917, this congregation was profoundly affected. Some 131 members were in military service. At that time its membership numbered 450 families."

Southern Jews have always taken great pains to look like their more prevalent Christian neighbors, and the rabbinic community did not particularly distinguish itself with bold, ethical leadership during the painful transitional years of Martin Luther King and the Civil Rights Movement now enshrined in the museum at the Lorraine Motel. In fact, King, while generally admiring Jewish history and drawing deeply from the Hebrew Scripture—especially the story of the slaves' escape from Egypt—once decried the local rabbi in Birmingham in the same way that the preacher often disparaged "white moderates." King was imprisoned in Birmingham in 1963 for "disturbing the peace," while police chief Bull Connor had high-powered fire hoses turned on adults and children who were trying to break the tyranny of segregation. In the municipal jail, King feverishly wrote the classic "Letter from the Birmingham City Jail" to eight clergymen—Micah Greenstein's professional predecessors—on newspaper margins, toilet rolls, paper scraps, and finally a writing pad.

> MY DEAR FELLOW CLERGYMEN:
>
> While confined here in the Birmingham city jail, I came across your recent statement calling my present activities "unwise and untimely."

King was as angry as he was eloquent. The "moderate" white clergy wanted King to be patient and not press too hard on Birmingham's intense segregation tradition and vicious police force. In between the lines of King's solicitousness and affirmation, one can detect that Dr. King knew that the clergymen really wished that he hadn't shown up in Birmingham. The long letter, which appealed to Christian ethics and was one of the stellar pleas for American social justice, helped King garner the Nobel Peace Prize in 1964.

The Birmingham rabbi, though not singled out publicly by King, was acting in concert with the strong, if bullied, sentiment of so many judicious (in their minds) church leaders in the South—let Southerners deal with the Negro problem rather than have "outsiders" provoke local authorities and push the process too swiftly. The fact is that some Jewish leaders in Birmingham, Memphis, Jacksonville, and elsewhere (with the notable exception of Rabbi Jacob Rothschild of Atlanta's The Temple, which was bombed with fifty sticks of dynamite in October, 1958, because the rabbi spoke out against segregation and invited Dr. King to speak from that pulpit) actually resented the incursions of idealistic—and courageous—Jewish liberals who came down in freedom campaigns from Northern cities.

It was a difficult and slippery dilemma: Southern Jews, trying to coexist with their Christian neighbors, socially, politically, and financially, were anxious about anti-Semitic repercussions (such as the bombing of Atlanta's preeminent synagogue) being heaped upon them after the Northern liberals returned to New York, Boston, Cleveland, and Chicago. Significant indignation was expressed by some indigenous Southern leaders of the Union of American Hebrew Congregations (Reform), who claimed, in anguish and hostility, that the New York–based organization had no right to dispatch a program of social action from outside the South and without any responsible knowledge of Southern ways and dangers. There was no danger—and there was moral clarity—in Micah Greenstein's love of the Civil Rights Movement, and his affection for the authenticity of Negro spirituals, and his nostalgia for his father's social work in the 1960s. There was redemption for the intimidated rabbis of that era in Micah's energetic board affiliation with the National Civil Rights Museum. But it's much easier for him than it was for the men and women, lay and clergy, who were equivocal—sometimes necessarily, sometimes enthusiastically—during the days when speaking out from the pulpit about the fact that black folks are actually human beings could invite a reprisal from the community, an anti-Semitic reaction from the mayor, or a dismissal from your own temple board.

It was hard. The atmosphere in Southern cities was fluid and treacherous.

People had lived in these towns and neighborhoods for generations; homes were maintained, businesses established, trade done, synagogues and churches built. There was a certain white intimacy that bowed to the great woodlands of Alabama and the red soils of Georgia, from porch to porch, dancing, like the fireflies of the Old Confederacy, amidst the mint juleps and under the twilight of long drawls, clinging traditions, and polite understandings.

There was no clear right or wrong in all this, except the glaring wrong that had been done to African Americans for centuries, that had not been eradicated at all by the 1863 Emancipation Proclamation, and was unquestionably a blight on Judeo-Christian biblical values and the American conscience.

So I asked myself, sitting in the breezy dining room of the Peabody Hotel with a former Cub Scout who now led the mightiest Jewish congregation between Cincinnati and Atlanta: Does this young man actually understand all this, even as he tells me that "the National Civil Rights Museum is where I hang out?" The answer was yes. It was yes, and I believed him, because, almost forty years after M. L. King and my time at Woodward High School, the gleam of those days shone in his face. Micah knew the names that mattered, the ideas that inspired, as well as some of the very people in Memphis, now aging and pensive, who knew the principals in the drama that sent both bright and burning sunbeams into the halls and classrooms of my high school when Micah was barely five years old. Micah helped me believe that what happened then still matters now.

A further note: After the paternalism of Ronald Reagan towards blacks, after the indifference of the Bushes and the manipulation of the black electorate by Bill Clinton, and after the ethical vacuity of such caricatures as black "activist" Al Sharpton and the venom of the likes of Nation of Islam minister Louis Farrakhan, there is really nothing political to be gained for a clergyperson to espouse the Movement—just as there was a lot to be lost back then for any such leader to embrace it. Then and now, spiritual leaders have identified with M. L. King because something stirred within them, not around them. President George W. Bush never addressed the national gathering of the NAACP until mid-2006; few people believe that former president Bill Clinton's comfortable residency in Harlem is not politically motivated. It took heart to say, with the striking Memphis garbage workers that drew Dr. King down in 1968, "I Am A Man." It took conviction to actually see those husbands, brothers, and sons—denied benefits, pensions, minimum wage, or even places to stand under cover when it rained—not as the "walking buzzards" they were called, but as American workers with their place in our society.

"After Dayton," Micah told me, "my Dad became a rabbi in Jacksonville. I tagged along with him to different churches. I was most moved in the black churches. I still feel this way. I listen to black gospel music and attend black churches when I have a free Sunday. I feel at home there. Something in their way touches me as a Jew. They celebrate faith and joy and gratitude. It's not about fear and guilt. I love Dr. King, not just his thoughts and intellect, but his approach to religion itself. I hear a voice in King as sensitive to the complexities and enormities of evil as anything I've ever known. He makes me feel Jewish."

"So it was good to be the only white Cub Scout?" I offered. We both laughed and I remembered the Band Room, the Ville, the statue of William Woodward, and the hard-won promise of my high school that I felt was being validated that morning while businesspeople, men and women, made deals in the Peabody Hotel, ducks lined up, and two rabbis from different eras found a common liturgy along the great oaks, magnolias, and pecan groves that align gracefully southward from Memphis into the Mississippi Delta.

· · · · ·

In the weeks after the assassination in Memphis, a relative calm, and a pall, returned to Woodward High School. Attention was turning to the presidential election (Dr. King had spurned some collegial attempts to encourage him to run himself), and awareness was shifting to the possible ethical vaccination of America being offered by Senator Robert F. Kennedy. RFK was clearly affected by the country's social illnesses, the unprecedented urban violence, the rampaging poverty, the disintegration of our farms, and, above all, the inexplicable Vietnam War. Kennedy's candidacy was given life by the departure from the race on March 31 of President Lyndon B. Johnson, and by the vacillating tendencies of the original Democratic antiwar candidate, Senator Eugene McCarthy. Bobby's voice had turned from shrill to soft.

But at Woodward, we tried to look away. We wanted the summer, the liberating heat, the romances, the Frisbee-throwing at Eden Park, the cold beers, the convertible Mustangs, the roller coasters of Cincinnati's Coney Island, the riverboats, and the sandlots. We were watching the improving Cincinnati Reds, particularly a nineteen-year-old wavy-haired pitcher from California named Gary Nolan. White as snow, but transcendently innocent, the country boy was hardly older than us, and seemed to exist in a zone atop a baseball mound light years away from the national traumas. Nolan was just trying to prove his natural, if undisciplined, talent with some rawhide and a rosin bag on a green field in a rickety ball yard called Crosley Field. When we turned to the Reds that unsettled springtime, we were blessed with hope and a fresh breeze, and we saw in Gary Nolan a manifestation of youth, a blend of boyhood and bravado that was somehow stronger than the draft boards, the curfews, or the riot police.

Gary Nolan had won four games, with a fastball and slider that were unfathomable to the National League's lumberjacks, by the time Robert Kennedy was gunned down in Los Angeles on June 5. So we at Woodward were back to memorializing, and the time had come for an in-house requiem to Martin Luther King.

It was the end of May—the week before Bobby was murdered. Senator Eugene McCarthy had stunned RFK with a victory in the Oregon presidential primary—the first time that any Kennedy had ever lost an election of any kind. But the California primary, with its treasure chest of delegates, was imminent, and a victory for the New York senator was expected and could prove decisive in terms of the Democratic nomination.

As the academic year wound down, the high school seemed to reel with a second wave of bereavement and dismay. Dr. King's voice was grievously missed, and the finality of the assassination in Memphis began to settle in. We felt vulnerable. My friend Steve and I conjured up images of black rioters invading the quiet, buckeye-laden streets of our Roselawn neighborhood; there was reason to fear this, as militants in Cincinnati's black community openly threatened a national racial war. In Oakland, California, young anti-draft mobs were beaten by police with clubs. Soldiers and U.S. marshals threw back thousands of war protestors at the Pentagon—the venom of the marchers was so extreme that many of them brandished Viet Cong flags and some even wielded axes. The rate of crimes committed by American teenagers spiraled to new heights. Cigarette smoking was ubiquitous, almost a required rite of passage. LSD use rose, hippies colonized Cincinnati's Calhoun Street, struggling auto workers walked off their jobs in Michigan, Vietnam escalated, babies in Biafra starved, Apollo 8 prepared for moon orbit, Jacqueline Kennedy became engaged to Aristotle Onassis and was denounced by the Catholic Church.

On the PA at the school, we were admonished to "act as Dr. King would have wanted you to." Our teachers and administrators were as earnest as they were plainly frightened of many of us. Bonnie Kind—who was twenty-two when she arrived at the school from Cleveland in 1968, taught social studies, and advised the school's chapter of Council on World Affairs—remembered almost four decades later, at the age of sixty: "There were days when I felt my skin crawl."

Meanwhile, those African American students who had looked up to the martyred preacher (generally reflecting the emotions of their parents) wailed for him: "Dr. King is dead! We have no one to lead us." Others, drawn to the ghost of Malcolm X (murdered by fellow Black Muslims in 1965) or by the likes of Black Panthers Eldridge Cleaver or H. Rap Brown, were sarcastic, vengeful, or both: "The King is dead. We're going to finish it."

Somebody parked a white Simca vehicle in the front circle of Woodward's entrance that spring. No one knew who the owner was and why the car remained there—a simple, foreign-looking, yet strangely appealing symbol of innocent rebellion. We were implored on the PA to find the driver and ask him or her to remove it, or it would be towed away. The Simca remained, aloof and indifferent to drugs, war, presidential campaigns, or swerving buses. The nervous assistant principals deferred the tow. Somebody painted the initials "M.L.K." on the right window of the little car. Somebody else put some potted plants on its back bumper. A host of flowery decals eventually appeared across the frame. An American flag waved from the antenna. The Simca made us laugh, think of poetry, and calmed us. It didn't vanish till the summer, and many of us, black and white, believed that it simply flew away to the heavens when it was done at Woodward High School.

The public address system was used by school principal Harry Hannum—a big man, ruggedly handsome, tough yet kindly-looking, who had made something of a name for himself in the state-operated media. Hannum was the host and narrator of a number of somber, even graphic educational movies prepared by the Ohio Highway Patrol to help teach new drivers about traffic laws, automotive protocol, and the dangers of drunken driving. I still remember my cold horror, at the age of sixteen, watching the actual footage of the bodies of DUI drivers, killed in accidents along Ohio freeways, being poured into body bags. I liked Harry Hannum and thought he was a leader, but when I saw him in the hallways, I generally had stomach cramps.

Hannum had suggested that our in-house "radio station," WFAE, broadcast a commemoration of Dr. King before the school year ended. I was one of the four students who made up the staff of the public address–based station that offered school news and commentary every morning. Our adviser was a chubby, crooked-shaped man named John Maniple, who was also a drama teacher and carried with him a constant affectation and flair, and a warm eye for some of our female students. Mr. Maniple had dreams of theatrical celebrity, but settled happily for his flock and followers at Woodward.

A "Martin Luther King Day" was proclaimed as June opened. We broadcast theme music from our little basement studio adjacent to Room B4, including a choral performance of "We Shall Overcome" and Jackie DeShannon's trademark rendition of "What the World Needs Now Is Love." It was decided that the closing paragraph of Martin Luther King's haunting "Mountaintop" speech, delivered amidst thunderclaps at Memphis's Mason Temple on April 3 just a few weeks earlier, and already hagiographic, should be read aloud.

I seized the opportunity, even though there was one black student, the soft-spoken Tom Perry, in our group.

And then I got to Memphis. And some began to say the threats, or talk about the threats that were out. What would happen to me from some of our sick white brothers?

Well, I don't know what will happen now. We've got some difficult days ahead. But it doesn't matter with me now. Because I've been to the mountaintop. And I don't mind. Like anybody, I would like to live a long life. Longevity has its place. But I'm not that concerned about that now. I just want to do God's will. And He's allowed me to go up to the mountain. And I've looked over. And I've se-e-e-en the Promised Land. I may not get there with you. But I want you to know tonight that we, as a people, will get to the Promised Land. And I'm happy tonight, I'm not concerned about anything. I'm not fearing any man. Mine eyes have seen the glory of the coming of the Lord.

So many years later, Reverend Samuel "Billy" Kyles would explain to me that "Martin preached the fear of death out of himself that night." Indeed, the filmed record shows that King was saturated with sweat and relief as he concluded the address and all but fell into the arms of his close associates on the lectern of Mason Temple. He was released from demons; biographer Taylor Branch wrote about King and that melancholic oration: "His voice searched for a long peak over the word 'seen,' then hesitated and landed with quick relief on 'the promised land,' as though discovering a friend." To this, Marshall Frady, in his touching and frank volume, *MLK*, added: "In the tumult of rejoicing that broke out at this point in the church—as Jesse Jackson, who was there with other King aides, would afterward report—'He was lifted up and had some mysterious aura around him, and a power. . . . The crowd was tremendously moved, in tears.'"

So, a few weeks later, that same bitter spring of 1968, in the WFAE studio of Woodward, I wanted to read those words because they were already part of my personal heritage. I was by then wondering, as I still do, how could King know and speak so candidly about his impending death? And when I returned to Memphis thirty-eight years later and spoke with Billy Kyles and with Micah Greenstein, I came away with the oral tradition, originated by Kyles, who was there, who *knew*, and would wrap the bleeding King in a blanket less than twenty-four hours later, that a man had gotten up and literally talked his fear of death out of his system.

But it wasn't okay with some of my black classmates that June that I was the one who repeated the words of MLK's "Mountaintop" homily. "That should have been spoken by a black person," I was told by more than one miffed student. Clifton and I were only exchanging glances by that point; there had been no actual rupture in our friendship, but a cold river flowed, and there was no bridge connecting our souls and sparking the one-time spontaneous mischief. He had stopped coming to band class as the year wound down to its thud of a conclusion, and had commented to me, as we both happened to wind up one afternoon at the Ville's candy machines: "Raleigh Taylor is a Southerner, and the South killed our man."

I didn't need to ask him his opinion on my reciting Dr. King's words on WFAE; his once expressive but now suspicious eyes told me that I was a usurper. But I never have agreed in my heart that it was not my right, as an American, as a grieving youngster who loved a man with clear ideals and who actually knew more about the Constitution and the promise of this country than many of the Members of Congress who were coaxed by his gallantry into passing the great social legislation of the 1960s—while I passed through a high school that he would have understood. It wasn't black or white for me at that school, except on those intermittent days when forces larger than us, and a war larger than our elders, and a troika of assassins (not one of whom were African American) who took out a New Age president, a lyrical senator, and a biblical preacher made it black or white for us. John Kennedy was forty-six at the end; Robert Kennedy, forty-two; and MLK, thirty-nine. None of the apostles at the Lorraine Motel that evening of April 4, 1968, were forty years old—and their quest would basically end that night. They dispersed, slowly but surely, afterwards: Ralph Abernathy, Jesse Jackson, Andrew Young, Billy Kyles, James Bevel, Hosea Williams, and the others.

But Martin King was mine as much as Bobby Kennedy was Clifton's; when was a housing law, a school meal, a ballot, a book, a drinking fountain, a city bus, or even a baseball diamond made sovereign by color? It *was* for me to recite MLK's words; he would have stood by me, especially since I have bothered to remember and teach them.

· · · · ·

arrived at the National Civil Rights Museum in Memphis at nine in the morning. It was the second day of June 2006. Barack Obama was laying the foundations of his historic run for the presidency. Some 2,500 U.S. servicemen and women had already fallen in the second Iraq war (it would be 4,000 by Easter 2008), recalling the Vietnam quagmire in complexity if not in scope. Gasoline prices, though still comparatively lower in America than in other countries, at that point exceeded $3 a gallon and were still going to soar. The racial wounds of Hurricane Katrina still blistered New Orleans and served to undermine the national self-image. The question of global warming loomed and literally beat down like the sun as record-breaking heat was building up across the continent. Martin Luther King, Jr., was, for most Americans, a postage stamp, an America Online icon choice under "Occasions—Black History Month," a boulevard in every fringe urban center in the country, a high school, a Monday in January for ritualistic dawn breakfast meetings when civic strangers act like civil neighbors and a good sale occurs at the mall.

Gwen Harmon, elegantly dressed in a business suit, younger looking than the "fiftyish" she offered when I mentioned that I was fifty-three, greeted me in her cramped office. Harmon was the marketing director of the museum that comprises the former Lorraine Motel. A universe away from 1968, when the motel gained its notoriety and symbolism, Harmon was a classic professional: skilled, organized, smart, and Internet-savvy. I didn't see any other museum executives who were not black or female. Some of the greeters and all of the custodians were male.

Gwen was guarded at first, but relaxed when I explained that I was writing a book about my high school, Dr. King, and the civil rights era. I had noticed that men were deconstructing a large number of party tables and chairs outside from an event that had taken place the night before. It was a bit surreal for me, though it should not have been: white tablecloths and flower pots and microphones being taken down in the heavy, humid air, within full view of the balcony at Room 306 where Dr. King had been gunned down. The wreath up there looked tired, I thought, and the motel site generally worn out.

"Oh, it was a charity event for the St. Jude Foundation," Gwen Harmon explained to me. "It was the first time we've ever let an outside agency use the site for a gathering." Memphis, it occurred to me, really had three cultural icons that don't necessarily intersect: Martin Luther King, Elvis Presley, and Danny Thomas. The latter was the much-beloved comedian and sitcom star of Lebanese descent who was a contemporary of Frank Sinatra, Lucille Ball, Milton Berle, and Joey Bishop. It was Thomas who founded the St. Jude Foundation and its internationally known children's medical center located in Memphis, in 1962. His daughter, Marlo Thomas, television's *That Girl* of the '60s, has also dedicated her life to the merciful hospital.

Gwen was intrigued by my story of Clifton Fleetwood and what happened on the morning of April 5, 1968. "How long have you been looking for him?"

"Really, since that day. Saw him a number of times afterwards, but never really talked with him. He smiled a lot at me, but kept a certain distance."

"Well, we can help you find him. You know, it's not hard these days."

"I've done all the stuff on the Internet."

"Find anything on him?"

"No," I lied. "His number is unlisted and he's not answering any mail." That was all true.

"Well, you know what?" Ms. Harmon was very focused now. "If you find him, we'll arrange for you to have a reunion with him right here at the museum. Peace and reconciliation are what we stand for."

I was struck by her offer, yet found something about it that didn't resonate. If my old friend preferred not to even answer my personal letters, why would he agree to be part of a staged moment in favor of the museum's public relations? Clifton told me on April 5, 1968, that the black experience was not for me. He must have eyeballed me a short time later when he hobnobbed with the intimidating men in the Ville who dispatched the two girls to beat up those two racist boys. Clifton made choices—even if they hurt me, they remain his right as a free man in this society.

Black men should not be put on display to service even a civil rights museum. Even M. L. King would have preferred to be a grandfather in the twenty-first century than a martyr of the twentieth. History is not forced, it happens—and it happens usually because of momentous circumstances. Reverend King was a youthful preacher at the Dexter Avenue Church in Montgomery, Alabama, in 1955. If Rosa Parks had not made her fateful and daring decision to sit down on the bus in a seat reserved for whites, King might never have been recruited to become president of the Montgomery Improvement Association and to spearhead the eleven-month bus boycott—which quickly led to his meteoric rise, over thirteen years, as the moral leader of our nation and a marked man. MLK didn't have a choice, but because of his sacrifice, Clifton Fleetwood, my withdrawn contemporary in a new century, has every choice.

I thanked Gwen Harmon, and she handed me a press kit and a series of brochures, which was her way of acknowledging my validity as a writer and journalist. I began walking through the National Civil Rights Museum.

Considerable effort and scholarship had been used to make the exhibits vivid, informative, and educational to people of every generation. The full arc of freedom history unfolded: from the bold slave Dred Scott, who unsuccessfully sued for his freedom in 1847, to Coretta Scott, who married the divinity and Ph.D. student "Mike" King in 1953 and went on to lead and inspire in several categories of social justice, including women's rights, children's education, and the dignity of gay and lesbian Americans. The museum successfully brought the history forward using multimedia: artifacts, recordings, newsreels, and archival documents. There was a replica of Central High School in Little Rock, Arkansas, a site of confrontation over black enrollment following the victorious *Brown v. Topeka Board of Education* legal challenge to segregation in 1954; a "Freedom Ride" Greyhound Bus, singed with fire and hate; a recreation of the podium at the Lincoln Memorial, where Dr. King left the text and extemporized his immortal and nation-changing "I Have A Dream" speech; a particularly striking floor-long duplication of a Memphis garbage truck, uncollected litter, and humanoid figures of the "walking buzzards" marching and bearing their signs declaring "I AM A MAN."

I was in the actual "motel section," on the second floor, and took a pause. I sat down and looked out a large window; where I physically sat was once a room in the Lorraine Motel that had now been converted into a small lobby with restrooms. The omnipresent white '60s-vintage Cadillacs from the R. S. Lewis and Sons Funeral Home, sent to chauffeur Dr. King, were parked outside eternally. I looked up and realized that I was gazing directly at the V-corner of the Lorraine balcony, outside Room 306, where Martin Luther King lay dying at 6 P.M. on Thursday, April 4, 1968. The single wreath confirmed the spot, but I saw the blood leaking from King's jaw, his shoes caught against the railings, his friend Ralph Abernathy leaning over him, whispering, "Martin, this is Ralph. It's gonna be all right."

Blood dries, but memories stain. King–Chet Huntley–Clifton–Woodward–Mountaintop–Steve–Quadrangle–Cops–Bobby–Vietnam–Chicago–Cincinnati–I AM A MAN—I was unable to look away for several deeply private moments. Nothing else in the motel/museum structure really mattered, not the quotes from Gandhi, not the passing references to Malcolm X, not the replicated '66 Mustang that belonged to King's assassin James Earl Ray, nor the gift shop T-shirts and baseball caps. This was where, underneath the ledge of spilt blood, I finally covered my eyes and released the salt water of my beliefs and obsessions.

Gwen Harmon had asked me, almost two hours earlier, if I found anything about Clifton on the Internet, and I had told her no. But something was reported in the *Amarillo (TX) Globe News* in January 2003. A Potter County grand jury returned an indictment: "Clifton Fleetwood, Jr., 50" (which would match his age, like mine, in 2003), "possession of marijuana less than 2,000 pounds but more than 50 pounds . . . ."

Actually, I took no judgmental interest in this and hadn't even realized that such items are routinely placed on the public record. The other people listed as "indicted or re-indicted" in the Amarillo newspaper that day were connected to thefts, burglaries, drunken driving, and sex offenses. My only interest was in Clifton's ultimate well-being. Sitting within feet of where MLK died, I wondered if Clifton turned away my letters because he was embarrassed by any knowledge I might have of his legal troubles. Maybe he couldn't trust me, under the circumstances. I could be associated with a parole officer. Or perhaps I was flattering myself and the man just wanted privacy or just didn't remember me the way I remember him. Not all of us remember Woodward and the 1960s with such sentimentality. It's hard enough being a black man in America anyway; what does a middle-aged fellow who used to be a high school drum major and now apparently lives in his parents' house again in Cincinnati need with the invasive, presumptuous inquiries of someone like me?

The thing I retained in particular from the Amarillo posting was the fact that Clifton apparently is a "Jr." Clifton Fleetwood, Jr. This told me that his father was also named Clifton, which mattered to me, since I spoke with Clifton's father, albeit briefly, on the afternoon of April 5, 1968.

I had been home two hours—it was after the sit-in and a small, supportive, parallel demonstration at the William Woodward statue, which I organized and led. It was after the little terror of the Ville, the riot at Swifton Shopping Center, after the police, after the encounter with Reggie Denning. I was home, sealed in my room, afraid and angry, both missing and resenting Clifton *so much*. Looking through the papers stuffed in my desk drawer, I suddenly came across the crumpled green roster of the Woodward High School Marching Band. Frantically, I scanned the names and found Clifton and his telephone number. Without hesitation, banking on a thousand shared pranks and a sea of sheet music, I dialed. It was a dreadful afternoon in America.

An adult man answered, with friendliness. "Hello?"

My mind raced. I was nervous and decided not to just ask for Clifton, but to be polite: "Is this Mr. Fleetwood?"

"Yes, it is. Can I help you?"

"I'm a friend of Clifton's, sir. I mean, we go to school together. In the band, mainly. Is he home?"

"No, he isn't here right now. In fact, I wish you could tell me where he is. I'm a little worried about him." The man was so kind and seemed very happy to talk.

"I understand, sir. Well, I did see him at school today, before everything happened."

"What happened?"

I could have punched myself. "No, nothing, I mean, just that school ended early. I'm sorry about what happened to Dr. King, Mr. Fleetwood."

"I know that you are."

"And I hope we'll all be okay after this. My family and I loved Dr. King, too." I was looking for some kind of parental lift until my own father and mother came home.

"Well, nothing like sunshine."

"Pardon me?"

"Nothing like sunshine. Just keep that in mind, son." And the line clicked.

· · · · ·

lifted my head now, thirty-eight years later, in the Lorraine Motel, under the shadow of Dr. King's final breath. The balcony, the sky, the museum were all gray. The wreath had no color; the world was starving for nothing like sunshine. There would be no Clifton, I realized, but I still had Rodney, Bobby, and Elmo, back at the hotel.

"What kind of country was that?"

MEMPHIS | FRIDAY EVENING, JUNE 2, 2006

I thought about the Jewish holiday of Shavuot while returning to the Marriott that afternoon. The commemoration had begun at sundown the day before, just hours after my arrival in Memphis. The summer festival honors the fiery, spectacular giving of the Ten Commandments ("inscribed with the finger of God") at Mount Sinai, which, according to the old Scripture, occurred exactly seven weeks after the escape of the Hebrew slaves from Egyptian bondage. Therefore, Shavuot (which means "Weeks") appears on the Jewish calendar seven weeks following the freedom festival of Passover.

By the time I returned to Memphis, after a twenty-two-year absence, and in conjunction with my own search for a lost friend and for the spirit of Dr. Martin Luther King, Jr., Shavuot was no longer exclusively a Jewish holiday for me. The Torah was given to my people at Mt. Sinai, but it belongs to every people—that's why we are called "a light unto the nations." We were chosen to *teach.* Even back at Woodward High School, with strong Jewish and Israeli roots, I felt that MLK would have agreed with me on this understanding of Jewish purpose, which happens to be derived right from the Bible itself. Time and time again, the old Scripture exhorts the Hebrew people to be kind, inclusive, open-hearted, "because you were a stranger in Egypt." This is the Torah of Woodward—we are all God's children, and we are strengthened by diversity.

I had preached endless sermons at the holiday from pulpits across the continent—from Canada to California. I had blessed countless tenth graders being confirmed, as is the synagogue custom, at the Torah festival. But my formative years at Woodward High School, with its ecumenical harvests and multicultural storms; the social spoilage of the Vietnam War; my singing journey with the Cincinnati Men's Glee Club, with its crescendo at New Orleans and its heartache at Veramayne; my creeping inability to regard the Jewish prayer book as necessarily the last word on devotion; and my unquenched thirst for what the Baptist preacher from Atlanta seemed to know about God's open palm, all served to make this day my Memphis Shavuot. I paused at the doorway of the Marriott, at the trolley crossroads, looked up at the sky glowing with a low sun, and made a prayer for worthiness.

Walking into the hotel's "Trolley Stop," I immediately met the eyes of the husky, smiling, gregarious Rodney—who offered up my requisite seltzer with lime juice from behind the bar. How many hours had this jocular young black man been working this day? Rodney, though physically dissimilar to my tall and lanky Clifton, brought to mind the upbeat drum major nonetheless. We had agreed to speak this night after our morning encounter, and I felt mutual joy in our reunion.

He did not require a lot of prompting to tell his story. He was born in Atlanta, almost two decades after MLK died, and arrived in Memphis at the age of seven. "I was a football star," he smiled wistfully, "but dropped out of high school in the twelfth grade."

Why, I wondered?

"My mama was a crack-ass," was the straightforward reply. He was clear-eyed and positive about his fate and situation, but seemed to be blinking regret out of his eyes. His adolescence had been fractured and he had wound up living temporarily with an uncle in Minneapolis. There was no mention of a father. I asked him if he felt any connection to Dr. King, in this pleasant hotel bar just blocks from the Lorraine Motel.

"Oh yes, definitely, man. I've read all about Dr. King, Malcolm X, Nelson Mandela. You know, I got two little daughters and they come first." The self-proclaimed "sports analyst" became intense and philosophical. "Life is not going to be given to you. You have to work for what you get."

Like a postmodern disciple of MLK, an unabashed denier of the crackheads, pimps, and victim-ideology minority opportunists of our era, Rodney laid out his Four Basic Rules for My Little Girls:

1. Brush Your Teeth.
2. Wash Your Face
3. Fold Your Clothes
4. Control That TV

"Look, I could spend my time feeling sorry for myself, but then what would that do for my daughters? I had them and I love them. So does their mama, even if she and I ain't together no more. But nobody in my world is going to be no crack-ass like *my* mama."

"You know, you sound like Dr. King," I told him.

"No, man, I sound like myself. I read King and all them, and they make sense to me, but the books don't tell me what I need to do every day. I know we got it better now than before. Black folks shouldn't complain. We shouldn't blame everybody else. It's the way you look at things. I like my sports and I like the way black men like LeBron James and Michael Jordan take care of themselves. Ain't nobody stopping them, no white man, nobody. It's the way you look at things," he repeated as I gulped and pursed my lips and *heard* Clifton Fleetwood proclaiming to me, "Attitude, bro."

But Rodney was still preaching, still girding his loins and keeping his life afloat: "Look, man, $2,000 is a million dollars to me; $2,000 is like two dollars for somebody else. That's not as important, though, as the fact that I know we got it better. That's what I get from reading about King and all the others. We can go to the bathrooms, the stores, and we don't have to find a black water fountain."

He paused and looked up at the NBA semifinal basketball game playing on the screen above. Then he looked back at me and sensed that I was moved by his rhetoric. "You got to be yourself, man."

Esse quam videri, I remembered. "To be rather than to seem." Rodney hadn't been to my high school and he hadn't even finished high school. But he had graduated from something important, and he was more than most of us who had either zipped, breezed, walked, or run through that school: he was a disciple of a notion now ephemeral, and there wasn't a false impulse in his burly person. Rodney gave me hope, as I sipped on my seltzer and lime and he returned to his commentary on the game playing above.

· · · · ·

Hope was not a regular collaborator at Woodward High School in the 1960s, though it did appear in fleeting and quirky modes. On a balmy morning in September 1966, the open windows sending clean, invigorating air into the classroom, a short, round but firm-looking older woman with a long thatch of gray hair tightened into a ponytail stood in front of her ninth-grade social studies class. Jennie Fine was near retirement when she stood before my group, but she remained feisty and defiant. She was the unofficial representative of the kind of orderly, civilized world that had vanished sometime before the high school culture she taught and disciplined in the era of race riots and Vietnam. In her day, presidents such as Truman and Eisenhower were appropriately distant, regal figures who came through on grainy television screens and were heroic in proportion to the distance. It mattered a lot that Ohio contained eighty-eight counties, and that Woodward was the first secondary school west of the Alleghenies, and that the National Weather Service was established in Cincinnati. "Miss Fine," as we reverently addressed her, was not impressed by the advent of color television and the

NBC Peacock, nor was she intimidated by snarling black and white hoods who roamed the halls of her school. She didn't know the difference between the Beatles and the upstart Dave Clark Five, and thought that Ed Sullivan had lost his focus when allowing either British band to sully the Sunday-night airwaves.

Miss Fine brandished a thick wooden paddle. The kinds of prohibitions against corporal punishment that are now widespread were either not in effect or were ignored at the time. When you got paddled by an assistant principal in his office, however, it had some context. When you were standing outside your locker and Miss Fine, a diminutive Gray Panther with fierce green eyes and a wooden weapon, walked by and whacked your butt just out of principle, it was wild. When you saw her down the hall repeating that wallop on the rear of a six-foot-three hooligan with an Afro who you knew had plundered innocent kids, it was downright gratifying. She was indomitable: not one school gangster—better armed, a foot taller, and considerably thicker than this little old Jewish lady—ever struck back. Miss Fine maintained authority with a kind of invisible defense perimeter and an "I-dare-you" attitude that defied the sometimes scary throng in our hallways.

On this refreshing September morning, Miss Fine, her thick hair in a bun, gathered herself before our class and smiled with incalculable warmth. The corridor-cop demeanor was gone; a gentle governess in a long sweater spoke to us. "What is the most beautiful word in any language?" she asked. Musings filled the room; black and white faces all stirred about, intertwined, intrigued, challenged. A few lewd suggestions, involving sex, hallucinogens, even violence, shot around the class. Miss Fine stood firmly above the fray, enjoying the anticipation, even if it was flawed by childhood bravado or, in some cases, some plain dysfunction.

The older woman turned her back and marched to the blackboard. Perhaps it was her complete vulnerability that made her so invincible, in that sanctuary-classroom forty years ago. She had no particular audio-visual aides, and her salary and pension were modest. Her own childhood was rooted in the Great Depression and listening to Franklin Delano Roosevelt's "fireside chats" on the radio. She lived with her sister Bessie, also a spinster, and planted flowers on a small patch of lawn in front of their duplex on Losantiville Avenue—almost directly adjacent to my own house on Bluefield Place. Outwardly sheltered, she had a deep instinct for the world, a prevailing sadness about it, and a certain probity that matched her uncompromising belief in our futures—no matter what.

She mounted a single-step ladder, took a long, thick, clean piece of chalk, and wrote the most beautiful word in any language, in distinct and glorious penmanship:

Home.

"There you have it," she proclaimed, coming back to the front of the class.

And then Miss Fine explained why "home" is the most beautiful word in any language. Your home is where you are totally yourself, completely uninhibited, perfectly safe, and unconditionally loved. The room took on a hush as Appalachian kids living in Carthage were spellbound by the notion, black kids from Avondale crinkled their noses and shut their eyes in contemplation, and we white Jewish kids from Roselawn and Amberley Village took it in affectionately. It didn't matter then that we subconsciously knew of the gaps in Miss Fine's concept—that some of us in any of the communities were not so safe at home, were not always loved, and could not necessarily be ourselves in our very own houses. Goodness—just that school year, Calvin Bernard, a curly-haired tenth grader and an illustrator for the *Bulldog Barks* newspaper, had died of a ruptured spleen brought on by a beating at home from the hands of his father. The Bernards were an upper-class, white, Catholic family, and the dad, who was now locked up, had been an executive with a prominent local ammonia company.

Nonetheless, Miss Fine's magical inscription and her sweet homily about home brought out that part of our collective being, on a forgiving morning in 1966, that yearned for exactly the haven beyond our country, beyond our school, and in some cases, beyond our homes, that the little old lady in a sweater and a bun imagined with us.

The session ended shortly thereafter, and as we students collected book bags, lunches, and belongings, and made our way into the river of humanity that our halls became between classes, I saw Miss Fine strap her paddle around her waist and prepare for her next patrol.

· · · · ·

ndeed, the hallways were a running pastiche of jangly bracelets, oversized AM radios, cracking Bazooka gum, glistening Brylcreem, swishing bell-bottoms, spiral subject binders, slide rules, combination locks, random chains, and occasional daggers. We skidded through the Ville; we renamed teachers (Mrs. Bazell, the chic American history teacher, became "Bo Bo Bazell," and Miss Nickell, the astonishingly tall and gloomy English teacher, was dubbed "Monkey Woman"); we dealt for smokes in the bathrooms by paying janitors for the preferred Marlboros and Salems. We avoided the intermittent fistfights that broke out, usually between black kids, and we sometimes held our ears against the shrieking and screaming that seemed to pervade the air. We stopped at the fake *Mona Lisa* portrait that hung on the first floor—just to gawk at the latest defacement that had occurred, using the perfunctory cigarettes and bubblegum that were placed into her mouth. We scattered when Miss Fine, purveyor of "home" and punishment, came by—not all of us able to quite escape the sting of her paddle and the hiss of her hall voice.

At Woodward, Clifton Fleetwood and I made fun of Miss Ruby Compton, the redoubtable civics teacher, because she was gangly and outspoken about being a single woman and a professional. She was an accomplished and skilled educator, but her perpetual personal social status aroused shameful speculations on our part. Years later, I learned that Ruby Compton never married because her fiancé, the love and hero of her life, died at Pearl Harbor on December 7, 1941, and she decided to turn her empty heart toward the edification of city students. I've wondered if Clifton ever discovered this, and if he might feel the same little disgrace. I think of Ruby Compton, departed along with Jennie Fine, every December 7th, which itself is now linked with

September 11th as markers of our national vulnerability, our gritty resilience, and our orphans and widows.

In 1966, Lyndon Baines Johnson was in the White House, Martin Luther King was in and out of Southern jails for following through on his Gandhi-inspired acts of nonviolent civil disobedience, Idlewild airfield in New York was now the John F. Kennedy International Airport, Walt Disney was at the end of his life, Walter Cronkite anchored the CBS News, Lucille Ball starred in *The Lucy Show*, hardly anyone knew about seat belts, automobile air conditioning was a novelty, people smoked in airplanes, restaurants, and movie theaters. We watched three television stations (the local CBS, NBC, and ABC affiliates) using rabbit-eared "tubes," telephones were rotary-dialed, General Motors led and Toyota followed. "Liberal" was the winning label in politics, and Islam was as unknown as the moon was still remote.

The mayors of Cincinnati, Chicago, New York, Atlanta, Los Angeles, and Memphis—in fact, of every major city—were white. No African American had ever won such a mayoralty. In Cleveland, Carl Stokes was preparing to run for mayor in what was already a racially charged situation. He and his brother Louis—scions of urban Cleveland, and the best-known black duo in Ohio politics—were the proud sons of Louise Stokes, a sweet, simple inner-city mother who had a will of her own and just wanted her boys to be upstanding. (In 2000, I would help dedicate a new post-office building in Shaker Heights, Ohio, with Congressman Louis Stokes at my side, in memory of his and Carl's mother.) Carl Stokes won a tense election in 1967 and became the first black mayor of any major American city. But during most of my years at Woodward, while black youngsters were perishing disproportionately in Vietnam, there was hardly even a concept of a black man or woman holding a momentous position of civic authority, and there were no black Major League baseball managers or football quarterbacks.

Henry Loeb, a Jew who had become Episcopalian, was the mayor of Memphis in those years. He had been confirmed at Micah Greenstein's Temple Israel as a tenth grader, but chose Christianity as a socially and politically ambitious adult. Strapping, handsome, Henry Loeb patronized the right country clubs in the mid '60s and, while not dispassionate altogether about the underprivileged, he maintained a distinct paternalism toward Memphis's blacks. Clifton and I were not aware of Memphis and its mayor in our Cincinnati high school until the spring of 1968, when a long-running labor dispute between the city and its overwhelmingly black sanitation workers began to gain national attention. In the back of Room B4 one morning, Clifton mentioned to me that Dr. King was planning to spend some time in Memphis.

King had not been heard from a great deal after a disastrous protest campaign in Chicago in mid-1967. The reverend had been deeply shaken by the visceral racial contempt heaped upon him and his associates when they came to Chicago to promote the rights of black tenants and consumers. White men and women, the men bare-chested in the heat and the women showing fangs, waved fists and shouted, "Go home, nigger!" Their kids joined them as they heaped wave upon wave of epithets, threats, and stones upon the civil rights leader. The Chicago city administration, led by Mayor Richard Daley, Sr., winked. Rev. King, prone to depression, sunk to new depths—even as he feared an assassination attempt at every corner. The North was more hateful than the South, he muttered. Coleman Brown, a professor at Colgate University who worked with King in Chicago, told me in 2006 that King's flagging spirits did not prevent the preacher from staying in the trenches and walking with the faithful—in spite of the fierce hostility and real danger.

Now, in the early weeks of 1968, Clifton and I were aware of the situation in Memphis. Some of Dr. King's antagonists within the black community had begun to refer to him derisively as "Da Lawd." I heard black students at Woodward suggest contemptuously that King's time had passed, and that he really was just a conceited press-hound, anyway. I never got that impression from Clifton. Between pranks and band drills, Clifton mentioned that nobody in the black community stood up for King when the preacher had the courage to come out against the Vietnam War a few months earlier.

"So what can he do in Memphis?" I asked Clifton.

"That's not the question, Ben," my classmate responded. "He got to go, nobody else will. Especially after they laid out those two garbage men."

The several exchanges we had about the Memphis garbage workers represented the most serious discussion I had with Clifton during that early spring of 1968. He was referring to Echol Cole and Robert Walker, the two sanitation workers who were crushed to death in the compression unit of a Memphis refuse truck on February 1. It had been raining a lot in the city, and the two men, accustomed to inferior treatment because they were black, could not seek shelter from the rain in the sanitation depot. So they attempted to keep dry by standing inside the barrel where refuse was dumped before it was mechanically compressed. The account was published in the *Memphis Commercial Appeal*, and Clifton, the normally sanguine and aloof musician, was very focused on this sequence of events at the time.

The downpour, however, caused an electrical short, and Echol and Robert were pounded to death. They were thirty-five and twenty-nine, respectively. I spent time at the heart-rending exhibit—complete with a reconstructed Memphis garbage truck, strewn synthetic refuse, and a photo exhibit about these two anonymous heroes—while at the National Civil Rights Museum, on the same day that I talked to the upbeat barman Rodney in the "Trolley Stop" bar.

At the time of this flashpoint labor dispute, glaringly racial and socially revealing, Clifton Fleetwood was engaged and agitated. In 2006, Rodney did not have any knowledge of the Echol Cole/Robert Walker incident, but he knew from history that Martin Luther King came to Memphis because of the ensuing dispute between the white Memphis hierarchy and 1,100 garbage men, almost all black, who were grossly underpaid and had no access to union protection on any level. As it turned out, they didn't even have a place to stand when it rained and, in fact, were sent home without pay if it did rain on any given Memphis day. All this Clifton knew in 1968, when we were tenth graders, and we frolicked at school, grabbed smokes, cut chemistry class in favor of something tasty at the Honeycomb, watched girls, avoided Jennie Fine's paddle, and analyzed the rising Cincinnati Reds. Yet both of us knew that something prickly stirred just under our skins.

So I originally learned about Echol Cole and Robert Walker from Clifton

Fleetwood. Years later, I saw them memorialized in a heartbreaking Los Angeles theatrical production entitled *I Am A Man!* by the playwright Oyamo. They were the infamous "walking buzzards," these two—and another one thousand black garbage collectors who pulled Dr. King away from his planning sessions for the 1968 Poor People's Campaign in Washington, DC, which he never saw. Their average pay in Memphis that year was $1.80 an hour. They were granted only leaky barrels to lift into poorly serviced, even decrepit trucks, and they had no place to take a coffee break, no personnel bathrooms, no pension. According to research done by Wayne State University, the "walking buzzards" were generally so wage-poor that a majority qualified for welfare and often took second jobs just to purchase food for their children and pay their rent. This was in the United States in 1968—twenty-three years after America led the defeat of European and Japanese fascism, and 105 years after President Abraham Lincoln's Emancipation Proclamation.

For their pointless deaths, the families of Echol Cole and Robert Walker were given a month's pay and $500 each for funeral expenses. Neither Mayor Henry Loeb nor any city officials chose to attend the funerals of these men, and no further compensation of any kind was ever extended. As a Baptist colleague of mine once said to a gathering of Jewish veterans of the Civil Rights Movement that I attended in Cleveland, "We've all had our own Egypt." It's been the same biblical cycle—from the Hebrews, to the early Christians, to the walking buzzards, to the children of Darfur.

Ten days after the gruesome deaths of Cole and Walker, the local sanitation unit of the American Federation of State, County and Municipal Employees organization voted to strike. It was February 11, 1968, and Taylor Rogers, an organizer of Local 1733, declared: "If you bend your back, people can ride it. But if you stand up straight, people can't ride your back. And that's what we did. We stood up straight."

The "I Am A Man" campaign began, arduously, valiantly. In Atlanta, at the headquarters of the Southern Christian Leadership Conference, the president, Rev. Martin Luther King, Jr., took heed. In Cincinnati, Clifton Fleetwood, drum major of the marching band and a tenth grader, took note and discussed it with a few friends. In the end, there was a bittersweet link between the doomed preacher, the impressionable percussionist, and a sleeping nation that would also be crushed in a national compressor that short-circuited.

· · · · ·

"Kids today, they don't know King." I had left Rodney in the pleasant bar area and kept my rendezvous with Elmo, a sinewy doorman in his early sixties whom I had befriended almost immediately after my arrival at the hotel in Memphis a day earlier. Now we stood at the concierge plaza; Elmo, very conscientious, spoke with me heartily but kept an eye open for people who might need him.

"They don't know nothing but what their parents tell them, if they are even listening. They don't know what I did in Vietnam or what King did here." His face was grizzled and charcoal-like, but he was quite handsome and his eyes shone bright through decades of hard experience.

"What was it like in Vietnam, especially for a black man?" I asked Elmo.

"Oh, we was all together, black and white," he said. "Wasn't like World War Two." He went on to describe, almost nostalgically it seemed, the rich green lands of Indochina. He was fascinated with the overabundant snakes and scorpions. It appeared to have been an adventure of sorts for a poor, if resourceful man born black and without a lot of advantages just after the end of the Second World War. Elmo relished describing the wild monkeys and dogs of Vietnam, adding, "They ate monkeys over there, oh yeah, all the time."

If Elmo had made a peace of sorts with his Vietnam days, even exalting the otherworldly, exotic quality of his Asian journey, his awe ended with his return stateside.

"I came back to Memphis in '68 because my grandmother died. I was here when King was shot. Oh man, they shut down the city, put everybody black and poor, the homeless, into the shelters. Big one at Poplar. They put the city under martial law and there was a curfew for two, three weeks, every night, six P.M. till six in the morning. You walked around, you got shot. I saw a couple of men get killed by the police. They was just trying to get home.

"I was a veteran, see, so I went outside in my uniform, so I was okay. Had to get some milk and food. I needed a job, so I went to the unemployment office wearing my army uniform. Things were ugly because King was dead and everybody was angry. But that wasn't the problem, see. People just spit on me because of the uniform. The unemployment lady said to me, 'You were killing babies in Vietnam, to hell with you.' It crushed me. I couldn't believe it. I could not get a job because not everybody wanted a young black man, thinking I wanted revenge for King, and everybody else hated me because I had been in Vietnam. What kind of country was that?"

· · · · ·

That night I dreamed of Clifton. He was walking in the desert—inexplicably, since he was returning to his house from Woodward High School. But this was the biblical wilderness, and Clifton had taken on the persona of the youthful Jacob who took flight in the desert after a dreadful falling-out with his brother Esau. Martin Luther King appeared in the twilight and showed Clifton a rock upon which to lay his head and rest. Clifton informally thanked King, addressing him as "Mike." I kept thinking in the dream that I would have *loved* to call MLK "Mike," as only his family or working intimates did—especially his brother A. D. or Ralph Abernathy. Only Clifton would have the gumption, I thought, to do that. I approached Clifton in the desert, under glittering starshine. MLK was gone, but it was truly an inviting, bright night. Clifton woke up and turned to me, his eyes small and menacing. "No man, this is not for you." Repulsed and devastated, I stepped back, as a ladder appeared from the heavens and extended to the sand. I expected angels to ascend and descend, as in the biblical story. It was a vertical convoy of monkey carcasses instead. I woke up suddenly, my heart attempting to flee my chest via my throat. "Mike King," I said out loud, while stumbling frantically across the dark Memphis hotel room into the bathroom for a glass of water.

. . . . .

n the morning, I waited for my car in the front circle, under cool sunshine. Bobby—tall like Elmo, also sixtyish, but broader than the Vietnam veteran—was my bellman. As the car was brought around, I motioned to the young man driving it to simply park it. Bobby was garrulous and outgoing, and he told me, almost casually, "I saw it happen at the Lorraine." His eyes moistened and his expression hardened, and I knew he was telling me facts.

"Tell me about it," I said.

"I worked nights at the Veterans Hospital on Jefferson, you know, cleaning up, but I lived on Huling. Right nearby the Lorraine. I actually wanted to see King that evening, you know, even from the distance, just to give me a lift. I was tired, didn't get much sleep during the day because I also pumped gas most days at the Texaco, you know, over nearby on Second. I was walking by the Lorraine and saw it. Heard the shots. It was so shocking."

According to every account, there had only been the one, desperately devastating shot fired, but I was not about to correct Bobby.

"Did the police talk to you?" I asked. He was sad-faced, resigned to something, and his whole body language was servile and shuffling, but there was something boiling within his frame.

"Police?" He laughed, pronouncing the word with Southern contempt, emphasizing the "o" in Police. "They didn't want to talk to any of us. There was bedlam all around there and they didn't want *us* around."

Bobby stared briefly into the morning sky. April 4, 1968, was a long time ago, yet he appeared to be looking right at it. He was born to a mother who surely loved him in an America that disregarded him, did not intend to have him schooled, vote, own property, or dream. I sensed that he was angry, but that even his anger had been burnished by time, circumstances, and the need to just survive. The voices of moral outrage, the rites of assertion, and certainly the expressions of black power that I heard and saw at Woodward High School in 1968 were not at all a part of his gestalt during the same era. His own adolescence had been one of accommodation, acquiescence, and remaining invisible. Bobby was probably sixty-two or so; Rodney at twenty-two, just inside the doors of the Marriott, was also limited, but did not define himself by his limitations and was not a stranger to society's possibilities. Rodney knew of no Negro League in sports, and he wasn't planning to work in a hotel or clean up somebody else's mess forever, and even if he didn't achieve his dreams, he wasn't going to blame anybody else for that failure, and he did not hold anybody else responsible for his fate. Two black men, footsteps and forty years apart, in a Memphis, Tennessee, that now as much resembled Dayton, Ohio, in both successes and disappointments as it did Tallahassee, Florida. Birmingham, Alabama, manufactured steel as much as Pittsburgh, Pennsylvania, drank bourbon. The nation forty years after the bellman, Bobby, saw Martin King shot down no longer officially distinguished between the races; Isaac Hayes maintained his celebrated soul restaurant in Memphis's Peabody Place, just a few blocks from the Lorraine Motel, while far more white people were on welfare in the country than blacks. Yet too many citizens viscerally believed that black ballots had been delegitimized in the presidential elections of 2000 and 2004, especially in Florida and Ohio. Few eyebrows were raised about the fact that so many cities had black mayors because it was understood and mostly whispered that the urban centers were black anyway, as whites had long fled to suburban subdivisions where once tomatoes were grown and horses were raised.

In March 2008, Senator Barack Obama found that his inimitable campaign for the presidency had become mired in racial issues. He spoke in Philadelphia:

> This is where we are right now. It's a racial stalemate we've been stuck in for years. Contrary to the claims of some of my critics, black and white, I have never been so naive as to believe that we can get beyond our racial divisions in a single election cycle, or with a single candidacy—particularly a candidacy as imperfect as my own.

So there was some kind of relative social equity, but we whites still expected our doormen and sanitation workers to be mostly black or Mexican, as well as our cleaning ladies, and shoe-shine people in airports, and teachers and civil servants in the inner cities. Woodward High School in Cincinnati, once a mosaic of social interaction and painful change, was now Woodward Technical Career High School—which meant that it was all-black and consigned to a new configuration that was as much a surrender as it was an innovation.

I asked Bobby what people felt most in Memphis when MLK was gunned down. "Fear," he answered. "Fear." He knew several of the garbage men, he added—"the walking buzzards."

"They felt bad, you know. They thought everybody would blame them for King being there in the first place. But they didn't talk much. They just tried to stay out of the way, like most of us."

I asked Bobby if he ever saw Dr. King up close. "Oh, many times. He wasn't a big man, you know. But he was a friendly man. Kind of shy, but very nice. Didn't ever stay at expensive hotels."

· · · · ·

I entered my car and drove to the Memphis airport. In my mind, I saw Elmo fighting off the Viet Cong in snake-infested jungles worlds away from the familiar, if challenging city streets of the nation he ostensibly defended. I saw Rodney, expansive and determined, analyzing the fluidity and independence of his basketball hero, LeBron James. I saw Bobby, the ruminative bellman, talking to a nameless garbage man beneath the shadows of 2nd and Vance Streets, sharing futility, fearing the blood at the Lorraine Motel, as though it was their own fault that America was still sifting through the soot and ashes of its Civil War in 1968. I saw Clifton Fleetwood, skinny and in free flight across the Woodward gridiron, leading me and the entire marching band, shaking off the rain-soaked bones of Echol Cole and Robert Walker, trying to forget everything but his beloved music and mischief.

In 1968, Bonnie Kind was a social studies teacher at Woodward High School, fresh out of teachers college, slight of body and formidable of mind. Decades after we all had walked out of the monumental steel front doors of the school, Bonnie summoned up her days there.

"I can recall as I was teaching there that I was fascinated by the socio-dramas that took place on a daily basis. The interactions between the many varieties of students and teachers of different academic and economic backgrounds were amazing. There was almost a 'crackle in the air' some days during class discussions and outside the classroom as well. I found it to be a remarkable teaching and learning environment. I would sometimes think to myself, 'This is amazing—but if I had children, would I want them to be attending this school or somewhere a bit safer and less controversial?' I never really answered that question for myself."

But it was not all so "amazing" for Bonnie and the rest of the teaching staff during those years when the school was a kind of national petri dish of race and demography.

"During my first year at Woodward, two of my students, one from home-room and one from the lower level history class, were arrested for murder. Both were convicted. One was white and under 18 so he was sent to a juvenile facility. The other was black and over 18, although still in tenth grade History, so he went to prison. He was actually taken from my classroom by the police."

Bonnie Kind, in her early twenties then, passionate about teaching, advising the Woodward chapter of the Council on World Affairs, developing her own social life, contended with many other things.

"I am sure you remember," she told me, "that there were three or four armed policemen in the school. In the teachers' lunchroom, they would remove their jackets and their guns were visible. There was also a full-time fireman in the building. And I remember one of the assistant principals said to me that he often thought about moving to Australia to avoid some of the problems. He liked their immigration policies."

When Bonnie quietly shared this anecdote and, in her characteristically mild and magnanimous fashion, indicated her reluctance to reveal such a flagrant attitude on the part of a high school administrator in 1968, I told her that this information, in particular the "I ought to be shipped over to Australia" mindset of that individual, was widely known by us students at the time. It only contributed to the thick tension that sometimes boiled over in the school and exacerbated the anxieties of so many students from both races. It was an incendiary reality that freed the more malicious misfits, white and black, to pursue their wicked intentions.

Bonnie had more to tell me:

> I also was sexually assaulted once after hours by a black student. I had stayed late to attend a swim meet at a student's request. It was not a serious assault, it could have been a lot worse. When I reported it to the assistant principal, who was black, incidentally, he said that I was one of several teachers who had made a similar report, same description of the student, same situation, and all that. He said that they had not warned the teachers because they did not want them to be worried. My thought was perhaps it would have been better for us to know so we could have been more vigilant. Wow, I have not thought about that for decades.
>
> One other thing just came to mind. I had a very difficult student and went to an assistant principal to express my concern. He told me that no one else had any difficulty with that particular student, so it was perhaps me, not him. I mentioned this to a few fellow teachers and they reassured me that this was the typical response to the newer teachers when they went in to the office with concerns about students. It was the principals' way of dealing with complaints that were not out of control.

Bonnie Kind was wistful and she wanted to put the best face on her memories. In truth, she had thrived in her few years at Woodward, made innovations in curricula and after-school programs such as the Council on World Affairs, and valued the mentoring she received from Miss Ruby Compton. But the way in which "certain problems" with difficult or dangerous students were dispensed with—the dismissive discipline, the chauvinistic posturing, and the racial stereotyping that was attendant on school policy has dragged on her soul. People like Bonnie Kind just wanted to teach about the Constitution, Raleigh Taylor wanted to make kids into musicians, Homer Caskey yearned to excite us about chemistry equations, and Linda Armstrong wanted us to find magic in Shakespearean sonnets. Without question, a segment of the student population, black and white, deserved none of these teachers' efforts. But when some of our administrators glossed over their own inabilities or racial prejudices; when they saw young teachers as helpless females rather than fledgling professionals, they themselves became a paradigm of the national government that didn't get around to reacting to injustice and inequity until—to paraphrase my brave tenth-grade teacher—things were out of control.

At some time during those momentous days, Dr. Martin Luther King, Jr., declared:

> All men are interdependent. . . . We are everlasting debtors to known and unknown men and women. When we arise in the morning, we go into the bathroom where we reach for a sponge which is provided for us by a Pacific islander. We reach for soap that is created for us by a European. Then at the table we drink coffee which is provided for us by a South American, or tea by a Chinese, or cocoa by a West African. Before we leave for our jobs we are already beholden to more than half of the world.

Wasn't MLK talking to the students, teachers, custodians, coaches, counselors, security officers, and administrators of my high school in the mid-sixties? Clifton, didn't you think so?

6.

"I was protecting you, man"

I awoke to a typical, blustery November day in downtown Cincinnati. Today I would see my longtime friend Steve, with whom I walked to Woodward High School regularly over forty years earlier, for the first time in nearly two decades. Looking out from my hotel window onto the city's trademark Fountain Square, it seemed that there weren't even any ghosts lingering above the one-time piazza of Cincinnati Transit buses and the venerable Tyler Davidson Fountain. The square Steve and I remember was being more than repaved.

A $42.6 million renovation was underway, of the fountain area and the attached parking garage facility. The surrounding area of grand hotels and department stores was being retenanted. A third generation of retro sports stadiums, one for baseball and one for football, had replaced the all-purpose Riverfront Stadium, which had uprooted the wooden and grassy Crosley Field of our childhood. Nearby Government Square—where Steve and I used to disembark from the BR43 bus to spend hours at the Cincinnati Public Library with real books and small pencils, note pads, wooden drawer catalogs, and the Dewey decimal filing system—an expansive multipurpose rink was being completed, over which a colossal outdoor flat television screen hovered with continuous football replays and summaries. The groan of cement trucks, the shrieking of moving scaffolds, the din of debris, the hauling, drilling, and remounting all smothered the quick footsteps of two high school boys who were looking for a few history volumes and then some chocolates at the nearby Mabley & Carew department store—which is now Macy's.

That November, a historic midterm election had rebuffed the administration and Iraq war policy of President George W. Bush. The sore allegory of Vietnam hung over the land, not meshing completely but resonating nonetheless. On Thanksgiving, a motion picture entitled *Bobby* was opening across the nation. The *New York Times* mused: "The sound of Kennedy's voice, even as it takes you out of the movie, throws you into a past that seems both terribly remote and uncannily alive." In Washington, a tearful Jesse Jackson and an overcome Andrew Young led hundreds of dignitaries in the groundbreaking ceremonies for the Martin Luther King Memorial, the only such federal site dedicated to a non-president and African American in our history. The comedian Michael Richards, "Kramer" of *Seinfeld* fame, burst out with a guttural, gushing spray of racial invective during a performance at a Los Angeles comedy club. He faced rehabilitation and court action. A leading law journal inveighed against the continuing bias hampering accomplished African American attorneys who are still denied partnerships in the better firms. The construction noise in postmodern Cincinnati could not drown out the undeniable echo of the war, politics, prejudices, music, and shouts of the 1960s.

Looking out my hotel window that gray morning, I thought about a girl whom Steve and I both knew back at Woodward High School. I could imagine her skating gracefully across the rink below. Debby Siegel, diminutive, rhapsodic, and supremely athletic, graduated with us and then disappeared, on quixotic wings, into the new world of divorce, Gulf War misadventures, and national materialism.

How Debby, a cheerleader, performer, artist, and editor, thrived within the atmosphere of that high school! Short, with a wide, appealing mouth virtually always in a smile, Debby walked briskly through the halls of Woodward with a certain good-natured innocence that defied any hostility or anger present along the walls. "I can't believe how much work I have to do—oh my God I am so freaked about the four exams I have in two days that I haven't even started studying for, but I know I just know it will all be okay!" She gulped the air as she seized me in the hall one morning and spilled her soul to me, the world swirling around her but unable to divert her from the full throttle of her angst and exultation.

Debby blessed the chaos and then flew above it. Long, frizzy, dark hair that seemed airborne, an oval face with forgiving eyes that declared absolute belief in humankind—I often teased this power-packed little figure that she was "the world's first hippie." She was not, nor was Woodward Woodstock or Bedford-Stuyvesant. She was, however, a nearly utopian free spirit who personified what we, in our best moments, genuinely strove to be in that time and place. The assassins' bullets that brought down MLK and RFK in 1968, and the approaching Kent State gunfire of 1970 would qualify Debby's good faith somewhat. She and I held hands and wept after we heard, early in the morning of June 6, 1968, that Robert F. Kennedy had died during the night following the shooting at the Los Angeles Ambassador Hotel.

As editor-in-chief of our weekly newspaper, *The Bulldog Barks*, Debby blue-penciled my commentaries. She stood by me when I wrote a particularly controversial edition of my column, "Kamin's Kontroversies," that took the all-black drill team to task for taunting the all-white majorette squad at virtually every football game. I lamented the internal school divisiveness and the racial undertones this fomented, and claimed that "racism is racism, no matter who is causing it." Debby danced across the stage in Woodward's annual "Showcase" theatrical revue, normally with her dance-captain partner, the leggier but equally goodhearted Greta Pope. Debby and Greta were truly like piano keys, ivory and ebony, and at the nadir of race relations in 1968, they grasped hands in rhythmic élan, and the smiling disdain of everything untoward and dangerous that crept along Woodward's halls.

I remembered Debby as I now stood in front of the empty Woodward High School, the great iron-like doors silent and sealed, thirty-eight-and-a-half years after Clifton had warned me, "This is not for you, man." A yellow sticker, the ominous cousin of "No Smoking" decals, with a black circle and a thick line cutting across a pictured handgun, was embossed upon the central door—a sadly suitable epitaph.

The school stood ready for imminent demolition. A mausoleum of blood and poetry, of dance and dread, of cheerleaders and drug dealers, the old building, still defiant in its silence, quaked adjacent to a newly minted, crystal-like, oval-shaped structure called Woodward Career Technical High School.

It was almost like a concrete wake, the young edifice attending to the old. My eyes ached in gratitude for this last vision of our turbulent temple, literally in its closing months before the wrecking ball—which would now be denied its final victory, at least in my mind and the minds of countless others. Steve stood near me while we recalled the social exercises of the front entranceway, the flirting, the fleeing, the textbooks heaving, the knives shining. We could hear Debby and Greta and the myriad of others, cheering, singing, bellowing:

> S-O-U-L, *Soul team,*
> *Sock it to me now!*
> UH UNGAUWA,
> *Woodward's got the power!*
> *Now say it louder!*

And then Clifton would appear, leading the pep band in varsity elitism, a perfect soldier of tempo and grace, bowing up and down to precise taps,

banging the bass drum and leading the way, with me and the others in tow.
We would chant:

> Hail to Woodward,
> Hail to Woodward High.
> Proudly wave our banner to the sky!
> We've got the spirit, we've got the fight.
> We're out to win with all our might,
> Hey Hey Hey!

Hush, this brisk and drizzly afternoon, a generation later. Look: Here is
the poplar tree that edges the grass hill out front. It was at this tree, right here,
that Clifton stopped me with his eyes that fateful morning. I walk along the
receding lawn, gazing downward at the athletic field—where the band often
rehearsed and the football team grunted in practice and bravado. Steve comes
up and reminds me that, as part of phys ed class, we used to have to run a full
lap round that field—a distance of one-and-a-quarter miles.

Now we see a solitary stone monument planted in memory of Peter
Johnston, a Woodward graduate, an infantry man who died in Vietnam in
1966. It was dedicated there by his family—a rock, a name, a war, a country
brought to its knees by the implication of this lonely marker in a schoolyard
where once a throng of scared and angry black youngsters poured out pain
and venom while the preacher's blood dried at the Lorraine Motel in Memphis.

Across the way, the shopping center once called Swifton—previously an
amalgam of five-and-tens, minor department stores, chili dogs, baseball caps,
photo booths, the "Honeycomb" confectionary stand, and stones shattering
glass. It is called Jordan Crossing now, a commercial property owned by a
faith-based group that includes the Allen Temple African Methodist Episcopal
Church on the lot where once we who had successfully earned Ohio driver's
licenses parked and showed off our GTOs and Mustangs. Even with the
synthetic, renamed stores and eateries, the gravel still lay and the air above
it hung broken and soulless.

. . . . .

My wife Audrey, who was with me for this pilgrimage, and who waited in the car, now joined Steve and me at the GI's marker as she shivered in the dampness. She respected the distance between her experiences as a high school student in New York City and the sepulcher that Steve and I now visited in Cincinnati. She sat in the back seat of our rented Subaru while Steve and I drove along our historic walking route from the neighborhood to our school some forty years ago.

We started walking less than a year after President Kennedy was killed in Dallas, and we kept on walking through the "invasion" of the Beatles; President Johnson's banner if incomplete "Great Society" legislation; the Gulf of Tonkin "incident" that dubiously justified American escalation in Vietnam; the indoctrination into our vocabularies of "Mekong Delta" and "Tet offensive"; Martin Luther King's Bloody Sunday march from the Edmund Pettus Bridge in Selma to the state capitol in Montgomery in 1965; the murder of Malcolm X that same year; the curdling threats of black separatists; Black Panthers, Grey Panthers; the ghoulish KKK murders of three young civil rights workers in Philadelphia, Mississippi; the catalyst rage following the bombing deaths of three little black girls at the 16th Street Baptist Church in Birmingham; the advent of feminism; the transformation to color television; the 200 millionth American in 1967; the race riots; antiwar and antidraft demonstrations; the draft-card and bra burnings; the Mexico City Olympic "Black Power" fists and MLK-RFK assassinations of 1968; the Apollo moon landing and the "Miracle Mets" of 1969; and the original Earth Day in 1970.

In between Steve's house on Eastlawn Drive and mine on Bluefield Place still stood Our Mother of Sorrows Church, where we (all white boys) often joined in baseball pickup games with the hospitable Catholic boys of the parish. The Jews and Catholics of this enclave called Roselawn got along fairly well; it was only our Bluefield pal, the scrawny and pale Bradley Hunt, who was ostracized in those days for being the only Protestant in the crowd.

We turned left from Bluefield onto Brookcrest. The opposite side of Brookcrest ended at the erstwhile Roselawn Shopping Center, which had once included the corner Center Pharmacy, replete with soda fountain and DC comic books; one of the first Baskin-Robbins "31 Flavors" ice cream shops, which once even featured "Jack Lemmon Lemon"; and the original "Hot Bagels" franchise store that galvanized the Jews and tantalized the gentiles and was showcased personally by Charles Kuralt on the CBS *Sunday Morning* television magazine as "an American place." Kuralt and Lemmon and soda fountains and ten-cent phone booths are all gone now, part of the hagiography of the once-benevolent Jewish ghetto called Roselawn, replaced by urban blight, pawn shops, and bail-bond and check-cashing centers. Gang members roved where Orthodox Jews once walked to the vanished Ohav Shalom synagogue, the Jewish Family Service, and the Roselawn Post Office. I noted that the residential streets of my old neighborhood were well maintained, and the church retained its grayish majesty and jurisdiction. Yet gone from the community was the sense of hope and promise that flourished with the changing flavors of gleaming ice cream, the steaming hot bagels, and the call of "Pickles"—the ancient, shriveled newspaper vendor who hawked the afternoon *Cincinnati Post* to the commuters returning in high-finned Buicks and Lark Studebakers from downtown, or the university-area hospitals, or the auto-building plants of Norwood, or the northern industrial complexes built by General Electric and sundry chemical firms. There seemed to be an uneasy civil orderliness where once I lived, fraught with a distinct edginess, but nobody was particularly coming or going from anywhere else.

We turned left onto Reading Road, passing the still-durable African-Methodist church with the daily aphorisms on its marquee. This was the corner where, on April 5, 1968, I came across the equally panicked Reggie Denning, who was also skidding home from the violence at Woodward.

Up Reading we drove, as I delivered a travelogue of places that had once existed and where now generic, unimpressive establishments ruled: the path to Marcy Greenbaum, the willowy majorette's house; Red Lobster; the Red Barn burger joint where I had worked; Mel Abrams's Mobil gasoline station at the corner of Seymour and Reading, where, across the intersection, the statue of William Woodward watched even now, in 2006.

On the morning of April 5, 1968, a few of us who were heading home in the wake of the black kids' sit-in gathered informally at the Woodward statue for a few moments. I had been stung by Clifton's rejection and then witnessed him briefly in the Ville, before the two tough black girls beat up those two show-off white boys. At the statue, along the edge of the frontier where Woodward's grass disappeared into the concrete of Seymour Avenue, we lingered. We were all white, mostly Jewish, and we felt the tyranny of fear and hasty exit. Though not black, we too felt sharp grief over the fresh murder of Dr. Martin Luther King, Jr. It fell to me to speak a few words of prayer. I looked in the direction of the fitful blacks that held their circle in the nearby front quad. My rabbinate was born that day in a rambling, somewhat cloying pitch for unity and affinity. I kept looking for Clifton in the nearby sea of bobbing heads, but he was not visible. It was my first public sermon, an adolescent flare, a sincere devotion, an undeniable root of identification with the people I labeled "America's Hebrews."

As the black crowd disintegrated into a rush on Swifton, and a few police on foot pursued, we fledgling liberals hastily fled the scene and ran home to our mothers and fathers.

• • • • •

The rain in front of the retired school building began to let up, though no sunlight broke through the heavy cloud cover. Steve, Audrey, and I climbed into the rented Subaru, taking in the welcome heat and looking out over the past and present through the intermittent swoosh of the windshield wipers. It was time to go over to Clifton Fleetwood's house and see what might happen.

I had the address; it was the same house in which Clifton grew up, and it was in the Bond Hill neighborhood just a few blocks from the high school. A generation ago, Bond Hill was Jewish and German—my pediatrician, Dr. Irwin Dunsky, worked from a building in the village. One of the brightest academic stars of our class, Jerry Nedelman, lived on the same street as Clifton. I had been to Jerry Nedelman's house several times, but never to Clifton's. I tried to shrug off my regret about this cultural apartheid to which I had acquiesced a generation earlier, my school accord with Clifton notwithstanding. Just a few doors from Clifton, I had cavorted with the white and Jewish Jerry, even though it was Clifton with whom I tried to fill an emotional hole for nearly four decades.

In 2006, Bond Hill was black, transitional, and had an unfortunate reputation for crime. It was probably an unusual thing for a sporty station wagon carrying three white folks—a stocky, tall rabbi; a thin, short NPR journalist; and a blond female businesswoman—to be searching for a house on Newfield Avenue in Cincinnati on a Sunday afternoon.

In my nervous haste that morning at the hotel, I had scribbled a house number from my notes onto a piece of paper: 5215 Newfield Avenue. Not two minutes from Woodward, we turned left onto Carrahen off Reading Road. I could see my pediatrician's office just up the way as we turned. Newfield came up quickly, where we would make a right turn. I remembered: Jerry Nedelman's house was just down to the left. How geographically adjacent to my own adolescent coordinates (we were constantly within ten minutes or so of my own house in Roselawn) was Clifton all those years, and yet how far was the reality of him and his existence at home. Turning the steering wheel, I also turned back residual sensations of shame and dismay—as well as a throb of latent opportunism.

Meanwhile, peering at the small, peeling homes, it became apparent that there was no "5215." Holy research! Here was "5213," there was "5217." A sure sense that I just wasn't destined to find Clifton settled in with a thud. I knew for sure that I had the correct address because both of the letters I had written to him in the previous weeks and months had gone unanswered but unreturned by the postal service. Other sources confirmed his address, and it was just his phone number that remained restricted.

I stopped the car and walked up to "5217." A wary older woman opened the door and told me that, no, she did not know any Clifton Fleetwood. While not hostile, she was eager for me to leave. I saw a skinny man, about my age, wearing a very dark raincoat and matching derby, walking by. Could this be Clifton? I approached him, as he chain-lit a cigarette between gray teeth. "Clifton Fleetwood?" He seemed to enjoy the oddity of my appearance in this neighborhood. "No, sir." I felt soaked and forlorn returning to the car. Steve suggested that we retreat to the hotel downtown and cross-reference my original notes.

In the back seat, Audrey, my resourceful and determined wife, was on the cellular phone with Cincinnati "Information." After being initially rebuffed, she convinced the second operator that she reached on "411" to release the correct street number of "this friend I've been looking for." She got the address; in my excitement, I had transposed the numbers of the Fleetwood home inaccurately.

The house was now in front of us. It was not unlike my adolescent home on Bluefield Place just blocks away, only narrower and frail-looking, without the benefit of any trees. There was barely a patch of lawn; what was there seemed barren and untended. I galloped up the walkway to the entrance and rang the bell. I could hear the football telecast of the Cincinnati Bengals versus the New Orleans Saints coming through the flimsy doorway. An older woman peered through a rectangular window. "Yes?" she inquired, without antagonism.

I was a bit dizzy with anticipation and hope, as Audrey and Steve watched from the car.

"Hi. My name is Ben Kamin and I'm a friend of Clifton's from high school. Don't mean to intrude at all. I'd love to say hello to him, if he's home."

A moment passed that seemed like eternity. The woman remained amiable, if cautious. She turned her head back into the house and I heard—to my elation—the declaration:

"Clifton, there's a white man here to see you."

And then a round face that appeared familiar, if inflated, was staring at me through the glass. A middle-aged man with gray chin whiskers, thickened jowls, receding hairline, but a recognizable glint in his eyes, smiled sheepishly at me.

"Clifton! It's me, Ben Kamin. Do you remember me from high school? I don't want anything but to say hello to an old friend. Don't mean to barge in at all. Is it okay just to say hello?"

Easily, casually, without a hint of resistance, he said: "I was asleep. Wait a minute, I want to put something on."

I turned around and looked at my two compatriots in the car. My thumb went up in a victory sign and I yelled out to them: "It's okay! He's here. He's going to say hello." I waved them in my direction, and they began walking up to the house just as Clifton Fleetwood opened the screen door halfway, still smiling, a bit tentative, but seemingly intrigued and amazed by the unlikely entourage of white folks and old memories.

"I was asleep, man."

"That's fine. Clifton, do you remember me?"

The one-time drum major seemed to be squinting; he really was not fully awake yet. His mannerisms—and his subtlety—brought back a wave of associations. It *was* him! "Yeah, I do," he smiled, though it seemed that his memory banks were recovering incrementally. At least thirty-six years had elapsed since we were face-to-face. Just because I had retained him in my spirit, written about him, quoted him, told my children about him, for decades—did not mean that he had carried a similar bond.

Audrey and Steve approached the stoop, and Clifton pointed at Steve, saying, "I remember *him*." He burst out laughing, because he was teasing me again, pushing me away while dragging me back in, toying with life, looking for irony as surely as he had found reprieve in the beats and measures of his sheet music. Beyond seeing the whimsical fifteen-year-old countenance within his weathered and full face, I felt the trusting, playful air of camaraderie emanating from my reawakening pal.

I quickly explained to Clifton about the book and his central role in it. "I see, that's wonderful," he declared respectfully. He did not appear nonplussed about being the subject of my project and repeated: "I was asleep, man. Watching the Bengals with my mother. I was sound asleep. I'm waking up now."

"Did you get a couple of letters I sent you, Clifton?"

"Yeah, I think I did"—somewhat embarrassed now by his apparent neglect of my inquiries. I did not want him to have any level of discomfort about anything, though I focused on not patronizing him. We had always had a totally unencumbered and spontaneous rapport in high school, and he was clearly falling back on that.

"Clifton, would you like to come out for a cup of coffee? We could catch up. I've come all the way from California. Can you spend a little time with us?"

Without hesitation, he replied: "Let me get a jacket. I was asleep, man."

In a few moments, we were all in the car and heading back across Reading Road—the traffic artery of our youthful adventures and the key surface street of Cincinnati. Clifton was too bulky to fasten the seatbelt and the automobile's warning system beeped at regular intervals. We three visitors solicitously ignored the strange and awkward situation. I didn't care, really, except for my friend's safety. It was hard to believe that, after all the years, the speculation, the yearning, he was actually riding with me, quite relaxed and at ease. Along the ten-minute ride, we made small talk about the weather, the National Football League, the vanished gathering place/burger landmark once called "Chili Time" (now a vacant lot across from the replaced Center Pharmacy), past the departed Avon Bakery, where my mother and I stopped for challah bread on the afternoon JFK was killed. Clifton knew of all these places—it was discomfiting that he had grown up so near to my own home, and though I had claimed his friendship, I never even knew that he was such a close reach away after school hours.

My God, I thought, what did I even know of him, after all? Through all those years, nearly four decades, I had worked in Canada, in New York, in Ohio, and California. I went to college and graduate school, was married, raised two kids, divorced, and married again. Who was he really? What was he, beyond a bittersweet memory that had haunted me? What did I know about his life, his experiences, his secrets, his disappointments, his children, his music, his career?

We were headed for Frisch's Big Boy, north on Reading Road, just beyond the confines of Roselawn. The Frisch family, who invented the double-burger concept and opened the original restaurants in Cincinnati decades ago, had maintained a "Mainliner" edition of their franchise—one that also created a landmark tartar sauce used by real Cincinnati connoisseurs on the renowned Frisch's French fries—in that location. I had spent countless Friday and Saturday nights in the '60s with masses of my high school friends devouring, socializing, cavorting, and squeezing girls within the confines of this de facto community. Woodward students routinely referred to the "FPL"—which meant "Frisch's Parking Lot"—and the FPL was as much a colony of the school as the Ville was an unruly province.

Frisch's "Mainliner," at Reading and Sunnybrook Roads, was named for a 1940s-era airplane that flew over the area en route to the Greater Cincinnati Airport. I have no recollection of any black kids being a part of the white throngs that congregated there on those giddy nights; now Clifton had selected the haunt as our destination for coffee and a reunion snack.

Even while walking into the once regal and spacious "Mainliner" ("They cut it in half since those days when we were in high school," said Clifton), my friend began to wax philosophical. "Life is too complex," he said to me, as if trying to explain all the vicissitudes that had deposited the two of us in our respective situations. "I've always liked it simple, and I just loved everybody. I didn't like any of the trouble we had back in those days."

I had told Clifton, while we drove across Reading Road, about the afternoon of April 5, 1968. "Did you know I called your house that day? Got your number from the band roster. I spoke with your father—is he still alive?"

"No," said Clifton, easily. "He died in 1989." He was listening intently. I relayed to him what his father said to me, after I expressed my concern and sadness about the killing of Dr. King and the trouble in the school that day.

"Your father was kind to me. And then he said something I just can't forget. He said, 'Nothing like sunshine.' I didn't really know what he meant, but I knew it was a kind of hopeful thing." Clifton didn't comment in the car about this (he never has), but seemed to understand more about the motive of my search for him that was culminating in this rainy November day in 2006.

Now, however, in a booth at Frisch's, in whose parking lot I once kissed

Peggy Sapadin—the exotic, Southern-bred prize from upscale Amberley Village in my embarrassingly staid '61 Lancer—Clifton picked up on the theme of that long-ago day.

"I went home that afternoon and took my time. My father probably was wondering where I was when you called." It was funny—Clifton seemed repentant, thirty-eight years later, that he had possibly worried his dad. He didn't dwell on it. We sat in a booth, ordered coffee, and, at my invitation, Clifton ordered a classic Big Boy sandwich and Coca-Cola. The restaurant, once home to white weekend throngs, now sedate and well-maintained, was comfortably integrated. Our young, upbeat black waitress, Connie, snapped a photograph of us and did not see anything demographically remarkable through the lens. In that moment, it was apparent how *successful* was the work of Dr. King, because even Frisch's Mainliner had been part of a long-standing social apartheid, still evident when Clifton Fleetwood and I did not mingle there.

"Man, there was so much trouble at that school," said Clifton. "Every time I wore those red pants, there was a bad day."

"Red pants?" I asked.

"Yeah, those damn red pants. Never failed. Wore those red pants and something happened at school."

"My God, I remember those red pants," I said, actually recalling his bizarre and flamboyant slacks that he did, in fact, don on occasion. In his lanky drum-major days, his pants looked like two flashy flags on long poles. It was classic Clifton—both the quirky recollection and the reality back in 1968.

Then I changed the subject to Raleigh Taylor, the band director with whom Clifton shared a symbiotic relationship. Clifton turned serious: "Taylor was Southern, man. He wasn't comfortable in that environment. I was never too sure about him." There was hurt and some resentment in Clifton's reminiscence, but, as with everything, the feeling was muted and he put it away rapidly in favor of some new lightness. It was clear that he carried the same vivid memories as me, although in his own way and in his own cadence.

Now, in the booth, Clifton basically ignoring his hamburger and keeping his friendly eyes upon me, I exclaimed: "So you do remember me, don't you?"

"Yeah, man, I do, of course. I was asleep before. I had to wake up."

"I've been looking for you for a long time, Clifton Fleetwood."

"Hey," he exclaimed, raising his hands in innocence and warmth. "I'm easy to find."

"Easy to find?"

"Sure. You found me, right?" Clifton was enjoying himself.

"So you're still in the same house that you grew up in?"

"I moved back to take care of my mama." He related to me that he had traveled about the country after high school, playing music—percussion—in a variety of locales and settings. There had indeed been a period of wandering, in the South and upper Midwest, along with a couple of marriages, children, and an abiding restlessness. He was seeing a woman half his age, and it fascinated him that she spent a great deal of her time reading and studying books in public libraries. He demurred when I asked anything else about his one-time married life, and he didn't offer anything detailed about his children.

"I'm not good at relationships," he told me intently and without shilly-shallying. He clearly loved his drums, and it was satisfying to learn that his immense talent gave him fulfillment and adventure. "I hung once with Lenny Castro," he mentioned, with obvious pride. "That man knows how to wear a pair of sunglasses. You know he played with Stevie Wonder and your gal, Barbra Streisand." My friend adored Ray Charles, and, he admitted, "I kind of have a thing for Terri Lyne Carrington. She's a hot-ticket drummer and *you know* she once played for Arsenio Hall." I didn't know, but was very drawn into his narrative. His road may have led him right back to his mother and to the house he grew up in just a few blocks from our high school, but Clifton had melody in his head.

Clifton was comfortable with everything, it seemed—his mischievous-ness, his quiet literacy, his domestic circumstances. He owned a catering and entertainment business, "Big Daddy's," and when he handed me his business card, he wrote his cellular number and e-mail address on the back with upright and clear handwriting that reminded me of his precision and standards in the band routines.

"Did you go to college?" I inquired.

"No, man, there was no money for that. No time, either. Being between all them walls, like we was at Woodward, that was easier for someone like you than me, man. Black folks don't always feel good in walls, in buildings run by white people. Woodward—I know it was some kind of special place for you, Ben. I knew that then, too. But it was just one more place for me to get out of, see. I didn't have no romance with it. But I loved my drums, see. You had a whole road ahead of you that was set up and that's good, believe me, I mean that. But I had to make the road happen, see. So I hit the road with my music and my drums. It was fun, sometimes scary. But there weren't no walls. That was my college, man. There were good days and there were bad days. I knew I'd have to be coming back to take care of my mama. That's how it is. But that was my education, you know what I mean?" He was smiling, enjoying having someone listen to his story, sensing that I understood the inexorable difference between him and me, even when we had run together long before in that high school.

I hesitated to ask him about what I once discovered in the Amarillo newspaper regarding a Clifton Fleetwood appearing before a judge for a marijuana charge. Nevertheless, as he rattled off a few states, including Indiana, Missouri, Kansas, and Arkansas, in which he had sojourned, I obliquely said: "I heard from somebody that you spent some time in Texas."

Clifton dismissed the reference, saying something inaudible under his breath. It was none of my business, I scolded myself, and I regretted my disingenuous diversion.

Then Clifton took his only bite out of the Big Boy hamburger and looked at me with convivial eyes. "I did get your two letters, Ben. Got 'em both. I have them in my 'to do file.'" His face lit up with characteristic self-parody. "You see, there's this pile. I look at it from time to time. Then things move into the file. Then I eventually get around to action. I remember you. You were always liberal. Always stood up for people. You're still a liberal."

A good trust filled the air between us. "Clifton, when the black kids came out of the school on the morning after Dr. King was killed, I saw you and wanted to join the sit-in. You looked at me and said, 'No, this is not for you, man.' I've been wondering all these years. Why did you say that to me?"

"I was protecting you, man."

"Protecting me?"

"Yes, protecting you. What happened after the sit-in?"

"You all went across to Swifton and started throwing rocks."

"Well, I didn't. I was protecting you because I knew they'd hurt you. Anybody white. That was the whole reason for the sit-in. They were upset about Dr. King, yeah. But it was all about going over to the shopping center, breaking up the stores, and hurting anybody white. I didn't agree with that. I had to go to the sit-in. But I didn't want any part of it because I knew what was really up. I walked away when most of them started running across Reading Road to Swifton. That's not who I am. I didn't want to be there. I just want to love everybody, see? I was never mad at you, Ben."

My friend Steve and my wife Audrey had been chatting amiably while Clifton and I commiserated about the past. But as I leaned back in wonder and revelation, I realized that the two of them had stopped talking and were taking in this bit of discourse between me and my classmate. I had a lump in my throat and felt some dampness in my eyes. Clifton was sympathetically triumphant, not about to become emotional, but he leaned closer to me.

"Don't you remember the other times I protected you? Every once in a while, I'd say, 'Don't go down to the football field today. Don't walk through the Ville today.' I didn't want you to get hurt. You see, you're a liberal. You didn't always get it. So when I knew something was going to happen, that they were out to jump people, I'd tell you not to go somewhere."

"My God, I do remember you warning me sometimes," I said, the picture of it filling my head.

"On the day of that sit-in, the ones out there on the grass, they weren't as worried about Dr. King as they were looking for a reason to make trouble. There was a riot at Swifton. I went back in the school and then I made my way home.

I didn't rush, though. Now I know why my mother and father were so mad at me when I got home! You called my house and told my dad that school was closed down, and they didn't know where I was. You're a damn liberal, Ben."

"So I guess you really do remember me?"

"I was asleep when you came over."

7

"Thank God we ain't what we was"

ater that night, in our Cincinnati hotel room, I phoned my elder daughter Sari, twenty-six at the time, in New York and told her that I had found Clifton Fleetwood.

"Oh my God, Dad! Clifton? You've only been talking about him since . . . well, since I was born! I have heard the stories about him since I can remember."

It was near-surreal and surely astonishing. Even more so because of the natural and easy flow of words and memories that was immediately established between me and my long-contemplated high school chum. Over the next several days, as I returned to California, Clifton and I spoke a number of times over the telephone. His voice was vibrant and affectionate. I felt a swelling love for him—the maturation of my keen fondness for him back in high school. He was distracted by his business, his children, and above all, by the care he administered to his mother. While it was apparent that Clifton did not receive much help from other members of his family as it pertained to his mother, he remained cheerful and accepted his responsibilities. There was always time to chat and reminisce with me, regardless of the many pressures upon him. We talked several times about the failing 2006 Cincinnati Bengals football team; they held much promise, but imploded at the end of the season. Several of their players were arrested for various felonies during the season, causing tension and bitterness in the clubhouse. The Bengals did not live up to their championship potential, and Clifton dismissed the team's plight: "No integrity," he sniffed.

I did realize each time that we spoke that there is an inherent goodness about him, and told him so. He seemed touched and promised to come to San Diego and visit someday. We exchanged greetings on Christmas Day and on New Year's Eve. Each time, he expressed concern for his mother.

Muriel Fleetwood died in February; my friend and I spoke about this as well. He remembered with grace and gratitude that Audrey and I had come back into the small house on Newfield Avenue on the day of our reunion to speak with and honor his mother. Audrey had placed her palms on Muriel's aged face and proclaimed: "You are so beautiful, Mrs. Fleetwood! Such pure skin." It was true—the ancient black woman, watching the football on television in her modest living room filled with her son and three white visitors, did look serene and stunning as the light happened to capture her at that moment.

I realized over time that, while Clifton was happy for me in my exploration of our high school and our country's recent history, and gave me both his blessing and his written release to write about him, he did not see our relationship in the racial terms that serviced my project. The friendliness in his voice, even when he was focused on his ailing mother, or attempting to parent his children, or trying to balance his checkbook, was as real as it had been back at Woodward High School. For me, the school was a paradigm; for him it was a school.

After we spoke for an especially long interlude on New Year's Day 2007

("I'm still going to get out there and visit you," was his wistful refrain), it occurred to me how truly considerate Clifton remained. He had immediately resolved my thirty-eight-year query when I knocked on his door six weeks earlier. The whole issue of "No, this is not for you, man" turned out to be about protection and friendship rather than opposition or rejection. After all those years, I now knew that on April 5, 1968, he was the most reluctant of participants in the sit-in in front of our high school, and he refused to take part in the rock-throwing and looting at Swifton Shopping Center across the street. He was making his way home at the very moment that I spoke to his father from the safety of my home that crucial day. Maybe the ambivalence that crept into our friendship for the final two years of our high school experience had more to do with me than with him, or even with our differing holds on Martin Luther King. I possibly assumed things about him and his outlook that were part of my cultural upbringing, while he was just trying to graduate. I was going to college and a profession, and he was trying to defy gravity on the wings of his music.

The assassination of Dr. King may have inspired me to become a rabbi. Maybe what it did for Clifton was to make him better aware of some of the limitations upon his future in America, emanating not only from white society but from elements in the black community as well.

To be an individual black man is not necessarily to have responsibility for the whole of black history. Perhaps I put some ownership of the racial crisis of the 1960s, so vividly played out in that high school, onto Clifton. I had no more of a right to do that than he would have had to ask me to own up to the Jewish agenda at that time. After all, Clifton never confronted me about the Six Day War between Israel and the Arab nations that took place in June 1967, and that subsequently created the Palestinian dilemma still festering forty years later. He did not define me based upon my youthful Zionism—although a few black students and at least one black teacher did. (In the spring of our senior year, 1970, this particular teacher prevented me from receiving a citizenship achievement award I coveted. She resented the Jewish militancy that I frequently declared in those days.) I should never be held accountable personally for another person's political views or biases any more than Clifton Fleetwood should be an emblem for a white view of black sociology.

In fact, Clifton chose to live his life thoughtfully, finding an existence somewhere in between the two poles of extremism and apathy. He grieved for Dr. King that fateful morning, and he identified with his community. This did not translate into a lust for lawlessness and chaos. He knew and felt enough to appreciate our band director's mentoring without disregarding Mr. Taylor's genteel racism. Clifton found his answer somewhere in between radical choices. If he were to meet the Memphis group of men, Clifton would probably admire Elmo's service in Vietnam while wondering about the older man's near-exaltation about the scorched country. He would relate to Bobby's friendship with some of the "walking buzzards" just as he had been angered and dismayed by the cruel fates of Echol Cole and Robert Walker in 1968. He would have enjoyed and approved of young Rodney's self-reliance and probably pulled me aside and said: "That's a good boy and he's got the right idea about being black and not blaming the world for everything you're up against. But he's a little crazy about those black athlete superstars because they don't care any more about him than they do about anything but making money."

During one of our long-distance conversations, I asked Clifton if young people today remember or care about Dr. King.

"No," he said, definitively. "They don't know history at all." He sounded dissatisfied. Clifton was generally philosophical, just as I recalled him from high school. But the whimsy was gone when he ruminated about today's teenagers. "What they know is 'Play Station One, Two, and Three.' They only go by what affects them," he said. He remembered that the only way he could control his two sons and his daughter when they were children was by the denial of television rights, because "that's what they wanted the most."

At the time, the media idol Oprah Winfrey had built a progressive, select school for underprivileged young South African girls. When asked why she did this rather than spend the money on African American youngsters, she responded that American kids only dreamed of "iPods and video games," while the South African girls, when asked about their dreams, longed for education, discipline, and school uniforms. Granted, the plight of the South African children was ghoulishly underpinned by an unrelenting death toll from AIDS, leaving an appalling number of them without mothers and fathers. But it was clear, watching Winfrey on CNN's *Larry King Live*, that she had been disappointed by the obsession of U.S. high-school-age blacks with Xbox and GameCube gadgetry.

"So Dr. King is really gone, isn't he?" I pursued my agenda with Clifton.

"It's all about fast food, Ben," was the retort. "Nobody cooks, nobody thinks. Life is complex, so the kids just go into their Play Station mode." Clifton chuckled. "Hey, you and I used to order a Whopper and a Coke. Today, they don't even say that. They just say 'Give me a Number 1, Number 2,' whatever. They just reel off a number and they are good to go. How do you expect kids like that to think about Dr. King?"

The journalist Pete Hamill wrote a controversial and courageous "Letter to a Black Friend" in the March 1988 edition of *Esquire* magazine. In it, he lamented the particularly rampant, deadly triangle of "drugs, television, and welfare" that was (and still is) infecting the black underclass. He took the growing black middle class to task for abandoning its responsibility to save the helpless poor, addicted, and homicidal urban core of black America, declaring that "Every day we see young people from a proud, tough race, nodding out on sidewalks or in public parks, wandering the streets at all hours, frequently homeless, or joined in the numb Fraternity of the Lost. I see shooting galleries, abandoned houses, empty lots. . . . These are kids who have been shaped in whole or in part by welfare or television."

In my search for Clifton Fleetwood, the words of that bartender at the Trolley Stop in Memphis, young Rodney, remained paramount: "You have to work for what you get," he told me, even as he declared his Four Basic Rules for his daughters: "Brush your teeth, wash your face, fold your clothes, control that TV." In my journey from April 5, 1968, I've seen hard-core racism, well-bred and overt, in the words and actions, in the politics and ideology, of so many white Americans, including the leaders of congregations and social service agencies with whom I've worked. Not everyone in the hierarchy was so happy with my regular pulpit invitations to prominent African American figures, such as Congressman Louis Stokes, during my tenure as rabbi of The Temple in Cleveland.

Yet, one conclusion is as inescapable as the situation is tragic: No American minority, be it the Koreans, the Latinos, the Italians, the Chinese, the Jews, or the Vietnamese has ever let ignorance become a virtue, nor pride become a rationalization. Most African Americans, including Clifton and Rodney and so many millions of anonymous, hard-working mothers, fathers, and particularly grandmothers, detest such capitulations. Their hearts are hurting for the vanished 30 percent of black males who are rotting in the ignominious American prison system, the shameless rampancy of black teenage pregnancies, and the 60 percent black dropout rate in our country's urban high schools. At Woodward, Bonnie Kind was dealing with nineteen-year-old murderers (of both races) who were languishing in tenth grade. Yet, Pete Hamill's magazine entreaty from 1988 still resonates:

> So I'm no longer surprised when black high school students tell me they have never heard of James Baldwin, Richard Wright, Jean Toomer, or Ralph Ellison, to mention only a few extraordinary black writers. They don't know that Alice Walker wrote *The Color Purple*. They have never heard of Romaine Bearden or Max Roach or Dizzy Gillepsie or Charlie Parker. They don't even know Aesop's fables or the Old Testament or the tales of the Greek gods. Go to a jazz club and listen to Wynton Marsalis: the audience is white. Young blacks are listening to the puerile doggerel of rap music. I find many white kids equally ignorant these days, but most of them don't have to fight their way out of the Underclass. Hundreds of thousands of black American kids are growing up in complete ignorance of the basic elements of Western culture *and* the culture of black America. Increasingly, they are not even acquiring the tools required to cure the ignorance. . . . Many such kids can't speak a plain American language, never mind aspire to the eloquent mastery of Martin Luther King or Malcolm X.

It's hard not to implore those in the black community who have prospered, who have matriculated, who do live in the suburbs, drive luxury automobiles, cure diseases, engineer technology, educate graduate students, and pioneer in other fields ranging from architecture to zoology, to remember the vast sea of impoverished, heroin-addicted, illiterate, and just plain *hungry* black kids who are as much the successors to the slave-genocide inflicted over four centuries on this continent as the black superstars who are shaping the twenty-first century.

This notion of class compassion is derived from the Passover story, recited by Jews, revered by Christians, and very much an inspiration for Dr. Martin Luther King—as he so often testified.

Every spring, sitting around the Seder table, tasting the bitter herbs of slavery and the sweet wine of liberty, chanting the freedom liturgies, we are moved by the biblical assertion that God "heard the cries of the Hebrews." This, after all, is what God told Moses directly—while sending the reluctant shepherd back to his native Egypt and the world's original civil rights campaign. The anguish of the Hebrews aroused a new spiritual standard. In response to the cries of the segregated and persecuted Hebrews, the intolerant Egyptians were punished and defeated via ten fearsome plagues.

But the Bible applies the same standard to the Jewish people soon enough. It's not long after the departure from Egypt—just at a time when the Hebrews might have wallowed in their status—that God turns the ethical tables back upon them: "*And a stranger shalt thou not wrong, neither shalt thou oppress him, for ye were strangers in the land of Egypt.*"

God even uses the same language to press the point. If the Hebrews oppress their own servants or indigents, and "*they cry at all unto me, I will surely hear their cry.*" God warns them, now that they have control of their own destiny, that they are not to betray the same prejudice that the Egyptians showed them.

The Hebrews did not always take heed (note the ragings of the Prophets, Jeremiah, Ezekiel, Amos, who excoriated them for their scorn of social justice), nor have modern Jews, Christians, and Muslims always been advocates for the oppressed within their own communities. The point is not to disparage such extraordinary, donation-fed agencies such as the United Jewish Communities, Hebrew Immigration Aid Society, Catholic Charities, United Negro College Fund, and so many hundreds of such charitable organizations from all the denominations. But in the case of the black middle class, a burgeoning demographic that reveals much that is good about our times, post-MLK, it may still be a question of something Clifton Fleetwood said a generation ago: "Attitude, bro." And as M. L. King said: "As long as there is poverty in the world I can never be rich, even if I have a billion dollars."

The difficulty with the view expressed by Pete Hamill and subscribed to by me is that when it is expressed, many white people take advantage of it. They renounce white America's considerable liability for the plight of the majority of African Americans, even forty years after King. When Clifton and I were students at Woodward High School, we heard, and he certainly *felt*, the degradation and summary dismissal of black folks. "They all look alike" was one statement spoken by a professional educator in that school. "Australia's immigration policies are worth a look," said another, aforementioned. "They just can't keep up with the white children," declared a lay leader from the parent educational committee—as if black children hadn't been confined since Reconstruction to inferior, unfunded, ill-equipped schools, and to the collective memory of humiliation at drugstore counters, ball parks, and bathrooms. It was just in the year 2006 that a notable and bright young Democrat, Representative Harold Ford, Jr., African American from Tennessee, lost a close Senate race to Chattanooga mayor Bob Corker. The most memorable, possibly decisive factor in the election: a notorious television ad run by the Republicans, showing an attractive white woman winking coyly and inviting "Harold" to call her—an unabashedly shameless bit of old-fashioned racial pandering. It worked; every black man in the nation, from those in prison to those in mansions, was defamed by this bit of gaudy stereotyping that is still acceptable in American politics.

In the milestone presidential campaign of 2008, when Barack Obama soared to the center of our national consciousness, racial tension and pandering clung nonetheless to the discussion, as vehemently as the issues of the Iraq war and the plummeting economy. We had come a long way, yet we found ourselves rewalking the path of 1968.

I met with Walter F. Mondale, the former vice president and 1984 Democratic presidential nominee, relaying the story of my high school and Clifton and my search for a reading on race relations. The meeting took place in Mondale's Washington, DC, law office two years after his landslide defeat at the hands of President Ronald Reagan. Mondale, long associated with civil rights and fair play, expressed a feeling of "regret." He could not attest to the endurance of Martin Luther King's dream; he knew King and stood beside him. "There is a kind of tawdriness out there," said Mondale. "People can't be aroused anymore about anybody but themselves."

In spite of all the tremendous progressive gains in social behavior and legislation that has occurred over the last forty years, I asked, why still this sense of polarization?

"I think there is still a strong, residual feeling in white America—with which I strongly disagree—that blacks should be doing more than they are to help themselves, that while the civil rights laws are all right, such things as affirmative action and so on are counterproductive."

And then Mondale was very emphatic, and he wanted to make sure that I heard him: "That kind of talk ignores the impact of slavery, and what two hundred years of discrimination do to a people. It completely overlooks the hard work, the patriotism—in peace and war—of black Americans, their spirituality and decency. It ignores the fact that so many black people have succeeded to the middle class and upper middle class, thanks to access to college and so on. We have a long way to go, and I would say that there is still that serious and often unexpressed—which makes it more dangerous—sentiment against black people. My God, if you take a poll, certain people won't admit they feel that way, but it's there, in their minds."

In 2002, at the age of seventy-four, Walter F. Mondale ran for his old Senate seat in Minnesota—a replacement for Senator Paul Wellstone, who had died in a plane crash eleven days before the vote. An emblem of old-fashioned liberalism, the former vice president lost the election to the conservative Republican former mayor of St. Paul, Norm Coleman. Though it was a close race, a key factor was the lack of memory that younger voters had for Mondale—and for liberal social ideology. Two years later, Harold Ford lost that Tennessee race to Bob Corker largely on the strength of racial innuendo. "We have a long way to go," Vice President Mondale told me more than twenty years ago. And we still do.

$$\cdot \ \cdot \ \cdot \ \cdot \ \cdot$$

Nicholson B. White was, until his retirement in 2001, the senior rector of St. Paul's Episcopal Church in Cleveland Heights, Ohio. An exceptionally kind, scholarly, and inclusive man, White developed faith and healing projects from Cleveland to Jerusalem to Haiti. He was active in the leadership circles of agencies ranging from the Cleveland Interchurch Council to the National Conference of Christians and Jews. We worked mutually in the Cleveland ecumenical community, exchanging pulpits and ideas while lunching and praying together often enough to grow a deep friendship. White was powerful in the diocese and well connected across many fields, endeavors, and national boards. But the most significant professional memory he carries is the appearance at his pulpit, on May 14, 1963, of Dr. Martin Luther King, Jr. White gave me a gift one day—a stirring black-and-white photograph of King, preaching from that lectern.

King was commuting between boycotts, demonstrations, police riots, and imprisonments in Birmingham as the summer of 1963 approached. In his comments that day, King called Birmingham "the worst big city in race relations in the United States and the most thoroughly segregated city in our country." At that very moment, the preacher was engineering a confrontation with the sadistic police chief of Birmingham, Eugene "Bull" Connor, a member of the Ku Klux Klan and a man unrivaled for his racial abhorrence of black people. Dr. King, in his classic, controversial strategy, lured Connor and his police into tactics of violence and mercilessness against silently protesting adults and children that actually put the Civil Rights Movement on the network news programs and in the national consciousness. Even President John F. Kennedy, while politically sensitive to his Southern base for reelection in 1964, took notice of the official brutality unleashed, with clubs, dogs, whips, and fire hoses, against nonviolent American citizens that dreadful summer.

"We have a long way to go before the problem is solved," declared Martin Luther King in the quaint and stately church of comfortable white folks in Cleveland Heights on May 14, 1963. And then he quoted the words of "an old Negro slave preacher":

"Lord, we ain't what we want to be; we ain't what we ought to be; we ain't what we gonna be; but thank God we ain't what we was."

• • • • •

Thirty years later, in 1993, a well-known American journalist introduced a new book he had written with the following recollection:

As a seven-year-old second grader at the Bernard School in McMinnville, Tennessee, I went to the compulsory assemblies where every few days we would sing this spiritual:

> "Go down Moses
> Way down in Egypt land
> Tell old Pharaoh
> Let my people go!"

I'd barely heard of Moses in my Methodist Sunday School and had no idea who Pharaoh was. But I got the sense that I was singing for the release of some people from bondage—black people, I supposed.

Carl Rowan, the author and journalist, was introducing his biography of Justice Thurgood Marshall—the distinguished first African American Supreme Court judge. I am certain that had I not attended Woodward High School in the 1960s, I would not have been immediately drawn to this particular biography, nor so keenly roused by Rowan's association with the Hebrew freedom story. In fact, Rowan wrote: "I would later learn that the spiritual referred to the Children of Israel but was universal in intent."

Clifton never discussed religion with me in high school. There were other black youngsters who did, and who cheerfully invoked such phrases, back in the 1960s, such as "Hallelujah!" and "Lord have mercy!" Some of them were intrigued by my Jewishness, or, occasionally, even scornful. "Ya'll have no soul," Ernestine from the drill team told me. "That guy with the funny hat who sings at your service"—she was referring to the synagogue cantor—"he acts like a fool. Just howling and howling. I don't get it. *We* know how to pray, and we put some feeling into it!"

I didn't totally disagree with her. Black folks do know how to pray, although some know how to cheat, lie, and hurt other people too, just as in any creed. Nor did I take umbrage at her liturgical assessment—we were both in high school during a frightening national period, and everybody was trying to figure out who they were and what that meant. The curiosity we carried about one another was a good thing; when curiosity dies, so does social progress. But when my friend exclaimed, "Land of Goshen!" one afternoon, I knew that Jews and blacks had more in common than most of us perceived.

"What does that mean, Ernestine?"

"I don't know. Shut up."

"No, no—what does it mean? 'Land of Goshen.' Is it an expression?"

"Sure it is, fool. It means, well, surprise. I'm surprised at something so I say—we all say—'Land of Goshen.'"

"It was a place, Ernestine. It was the province in Egypt where the Hebrews had to live. It's in the Bible. Goshen, that's where the Hebrew slaves all lived."

"Y'all always had your own neighborhood. Go away, fool. I say what I want and I don't give a shit about no Hebrews in Egypt. Wait, you got a ink-pen?"

For many African Americans, however, faith is grounded in the Hebrew scripture. They learned it and grew up with it. It inspired them through much difficulty and anguish—including the assassinations of Martin Luther King, Malcolm X, and Medgar Evers, among others well known and anonymous. The black freedom theology hails from the Passover saga of the Book of Exodus. Again and again, I have heard black clergy declare, from lecterns we've shared and in private conversations, "We both have had our own Egypt," with "we" meaning Jews and blacks.

There is much to be said for this important sharing of a tradition, especially in these times of cultural balkanization. After the defining days of the Civil Rights Movement, from the Montgomery bus boycott of 1955 to the Memphis sanitation workers' strike in 1968, there has been a lapse here. Louis Farrakhan of the Nation of Islam, with his hideous anti-Semitism and his many acolytes, made it difficult for some Jews—including some of my Woodward classmates—to remain committed to multiculturalism as we came of age. Nor did the moral upper hand always remain with Israel when it came to the Palestinian issue in the decades since the decisive and thrilling Israeli victory in the Six Day War of 1967 and the assassination of Dr. King in 1968. Jews were conflicted; blacks were suspicious.

Some of MLK's successors played off the Palestinian situation, linking American blacks to the people of Gaza and the West Bank—even if the linkage played awkwardly. There was something unconvincing about Reverend Jesse Jackson's theatrical performances in Palestinian towns, exhorting Muslim villagers to join him in the chanting of his trademark "I am somebody!" Jackson, by his sheer dynamism and daunting physical presence (I was one of his co-officiants at the funeral, in 1996, of Cleveland mayor Carl B. Stokes), can make a claim as Dr. King's public successor in African American leadership. Jackson, an undeniably significant champion of social justice, has made questionable comments about Jews in the past. Dr. King remained focused on the economic struggle of underprivileged Americans, and he actually dismissed talk of a presidential candidacy. Jackson ran for president twice, won some primaries, and seemed intoxicated by the attention. He did achieve something singular: the immense registration of black voters spurred by his candidacies paved the way for Barack Obama in 2008.

And yet—when one reads the Passover story, one reads about a universal yearning for freedom. This is something Jews and blacks do understand together, when both groups are willing to share. When I was a Woodward High School student, rabbis were marching with Martin and Coretta King out of proportion to their numbers, while our parents in Cincinnati and elsewhere were verbalizing sympathy for black folks during the Passover Seders of our adolescence. Many Jews would smile warmly upon Carl Rowan's recollection of the spiritual about old Pharaoh and the slaves.

Passover has always made me think about this tension. I think about Clifton, the sit-in, the Lorraine balcony, and my friend admonishing me to separate from his pain. Although I now know why he told me to leave, still I say, "Never!" I don't want the old Hebrew redemption story to remain static in the book, or to be forgotten as some ancient adventure that means little for my times, my community, my children. And in my lifetime, there have been triumphant moments, from Birmingham, Alabama; to Pretoria, South Africa; to Cincinnati, Ohio; to Berlin, Germany, during which people of many different colors have lived out the historical refrain of "Let my people go!"

Woodward taught me: We blacks and Jews are fused in American history. From Moses to Martin Luther King, Jr., we have been reciting some of the same poetry, we have been sharing dreams, we have found mutual strength, and we certainly have had much in common to fear when America as a whole has felt threatened by real or imagined social and economic ills.

There is a Pharaoh of the spirit that comes to afflict both of our peoples—and all peoples. Some individuals, even groups, uncannily blame "the Jews" for 9/11, or a "Jewish cabal" for its alleged control of the media, or even of the Congress of the United States. When a terribly sick white mother in South Carolina reported, several years ago, that her two small children had been kidnapped by a grisly black assailant, white Americans (including Jews) shook their heads in grave confirmation that the perpetrator was a black man. Yet there was no such criminal; the mother herself drove her own flesh and blood—strapped in their car seats—into a cold lake to be drowned. She murdered her own offspring, and continued the murder-by-stereotyping of black males.

I might have thought about these kinds of things anyway. But if I hadn't attended Woodward High School from 1964 to 1970, and been weaned off social isolation by its harsh and edifying reality, I would have not thought about these things with the same intensity. And I would not have converted any moral outrage, which is my high school legacy, into a ministry.

For me, Memphis is not about Elvis Presley; it's about Martin Luther King. I bristle when black-based theater is still referred to as "urban theater" (or pejoratively as the "chitlin' circuit") rather than as part of mainstream entertainment—as if every black dramatic moment or insight is confined to the inner city. Some of my most cherished movie memories come from *Driving Miss Daisy*, the Pulitzer play and 1989 Academy Award winner starring Jessica Tandy and Morgan Freeman—one of playwright Alfred Uhry's "Atlanta trilogy." In the drama, Freeman plays "Hoke," the chauffeur for the affluent Jewish matriarch Miss Daisy. On one occasion, he drives her from Atlanta to a family celebration in Mobile, Alabama. Unable to properly decipher her map, Miss Daisy misdirects Hoke at a key rural intersection, and their journey becomes delayed and tense.

The woman requires a comfort stop at a filling station along the way, where Hoke pumps gasoline but is forbidden to use the restroom. Not long after, he pulls over in the night and informs Miss Daisy that he has to pass water. She is nervous and impatient in the darkness and tells him he can wait till they arrive in Mobile. Hoke, normally even-tempered and cheerfully servile, finally protests—but it's not just about his full bladder. Without sarcasm but with contained anger, he informs the white woman that he is a man, and that he has the right to relieve himself without asking anybody for permission. The soft but powerful scene has always moved me to tears—without bloodshed, without even rancor, the unforgivable indignity heaped upon black men is expressed and realized.

I watched the scene with my teenaged stepchildren in 2007 and asked them not to take things for granted. I asked them to understand that things happened in our America not very long ago that tried the souls of enough good people to deliver a society that is far from perfect, but which is better. When the composite "Hoke" of Alfred Uhry's masterpiece can be himself, then every Jewish child is also that many more heartbeats away from the Nazis of just two generations ago, and every black child (too many of whom don't even know that there was once a problem) can just read about, and not experience, Jim Crow.

I understand now, forty years after April 5, 1968, the sorrow in Clifton Fleetwood's eyes that gray April morning, and I understand the fury that shook the air. Those kids had lost their Moses. They had a president who, yes, had fought for legislation that granted voting and civil rights to their color; but two garbage men had been crushed to death in a sanitation cylinder just weeks before, strictly because they were black and wanted to come in from the rain. The president had uttered, "We shall overcome" before a joint session of Congress in 1965, yes, but was sending hundreds of thousands of youngsters, so many of them black and unable to dodge the draft, to the Armageddon of Vietnam. America was passing liberal laws, but killing liberal lawmakers. America was no longer officially segregated, but in cities from Tallahassee to Chicago, white mothers were yelling, "Two, four, six, eight, we will never integrate!" So what were those black students in front of Woodward supposed to feel on the morning of April 5, 1968, other than the grief of having lost their Moses?

When the biblical Moses went into Pharaoh's court and demanded freedom for the slaves, he was speaking for every nation and every age. This was the first time in recorded history that any cultural nationality demanded and got a deliverance from the prevailing power. Moses was the world's first civil rights leader, and the Hebrew exodus from Egypt was the world's first national liberation movement. No wonder that so many Americans, Jews and Christians, identified with Dr. Martin Luther King's social revolution of forty years ago. And we need to remember now—because so many of us personally recall a turbulent high school, a friend, a sit-in, a protest, a racist teacher, a freedom song—just how much the movement gave back to us.

When white social activists made their way down to Birmingham, Selma, and Jackson, they were fulfilling their own idea of what faith really is. It's a question of turning history into ethics. The scriptural prophets, from Isaiah to

Amos to Jeremiah, were looking for a religious life based upon *acts of justice* more than empty rituals. Dr. King often chastised his listeners, quoting Jesus: "I was hungry and you fed me not." This was a paraphrasing of Isaiah's ancient cry, "To undo the bands of the yoke, and to let the oppressed go free."

> *Is this not the fast I have chosen?*
>
>   . . .
>
> *Is it not to deal thy bread to the hungry,*
> *And that thou bring the poor that are cast out to thy house?*
> *When thou seest the naked, that thou cover him,*
> *And that thou hide not thyself from thine own flesh?*
> *Then shall thy light break forth as morning.*

Indeed, the plight of black Americans cleared an avenue of pastoral meaning for many Jews at the time who were, frankly, not engaged by their Judaism. This was deeply rooted: in 1909, a disproportionate four Jews were among the sixty multicultural signers of the call to National Action, which resulted in the creation of the National Association for the Advancement of Colored People (NAACP).

Later, while we helped blacks to desegregate drinking fountains, to unlock the doors of state universities, and to open up voting booths, they in turn were opening up our souls and helping us to negotiate our own religious ambivalence. They—Clifton's people—became our unlikely partners in the realization of our Passover promises.

In general, it was science and justice, not faith and spirituality, that defined those heady days of LBJ's Great Society and the War on Poverty. Jews, and others, thought much more about the effect of the Soviet Sputnik satellite than they did about the impact of the Sabbath. When MLK took over the presidency of the Montgomery Improvement Association in 1955, the European ashes of fascism were still fresh in the earth, and Soviet teeth were deeply embedded in the continent. In the Jewish community, there was still shocked silence about what the Nazis had done, and nobody was really talking about it—or making too much noise about being Jewish in general. It wasn't until 1993—fifty years after the Warsaw Ghetto uprising—that Steven Spielberg made the groundbreaking and stark Holocaust motion picture *Schindler's List*.

While Spielberg was growing up in Cincinnati, the generation of pre-Vietnam, suburban-bound hip-hoppers wore saddle shoes to Woodward High School and listened to Elvis Presley and Wolfman Jack, while many religious people focused more on philosophy and Communism than God and rituals. Rabbis mixed quotations from Ezekiel with the poetry of Gandhi. They and clergy from other faiths drew a legitimate line from Pharaoh to governors George Wallace and Lester Maddox.

The chant of "Let my people go!" was not so much a scriptural cantillation as it was the political plank of so many faith agencies in the days that gave rise to Martin Luther King, Jr. The searing needs of African Americans, so evident to me by implication while at Woodward High School, provided Jews with an agenda—and a post-genocide focus. The plunge into civil rights was the schema of American Jews long before our more recent infatuation with rituals, with the Hebrew language, with Jewish literacy, and demographic continuity. We were even more interested in this than in Israel—until the Jewish state's lightning victory in 1967 against the Arabs made us feel proud and audacious. My ninth-grade year at Woodward, 1966–67, was a strange, compound din of black militancy and Jewish restitution. Nonetheless, the typical American Jew forty years ago knew a lot more about Martin Luther King, Jr., than about Oskar Schindler.

While recalling Woodward and my friend Clifton, I refer to all of this for two reasons. First, the awareness of Passover-inspired values, usually learned at home around a Seder table, clearly motivated many thoughtful Jews to participate—sometimes at real personal risk—in the modern American social struggle against the Pharaonic sheriffs, mayors, and governors of the old Confederacy. Second, given that Clifton and I were not typical in our friendship, and that there has been a waning of black-Jewish relations, it is worthwhile to revisit the rough parallels between the "two Egypts."

Blacks and Jews may both chant, "Let my people go!" but it hasn't been the same melody. When it was the Hebrews who were being liberated, there was a designated leader (Moses) and there was a destination (Canaan). The former Egyptian slaves were released into a religious tradition, and they were headed for a specific land inheritance. They enjoyed good care and protection. The Hebrews were released as a group; simultaneously, they were handed a series of defining laws and educational covenants, and they were transferred to a holy plot of soil.

"Let my people go!" did not ring so truly for the African slaves of this continent. They were delivered by an Emancipation Proclamation agreed to by only half of a nation embroiled in a civil war. There was no equivalent convocation following manumission at any kind of American Sinai. Black Americans were freed—to drift off and hide. Unlike the Hebrews, they were not given a legal code to help them become citizens, or even participants, in society. The cruel aftermath known as Reconstruction was hardly a redemption—it was collaborative, malignant, deceptive, ruthless, and reeking of racism. President Abraham Lincoln was martyred in 1865 before he could deliver on the promise of the Union victory for black people—who rolled over from plantation slavery into an unrelenting bondage of homelessness and hunger, without voting rights, property rights, schools, unions, or communal status. Blacks were segregated, lynched, abused, and despoiled while the Southern pathologists that ravaged them enjoyed complete immunity until a hundred years after Lincoln. While being separated from mainstream society, black men were nonetheless routinely drafted to defend America in two world wars, the Korean stalemate, and the Vietnam fiasco. As a group, the former slaves of America were not led by Moses. They were chased by another fellow named Jim Crow—the pseudonym for state-sanctioned segregation.

Dr. Martin Luther King, Jr., was not intending to inspire Jews to go back to their textual homeland of the Book of Exodus and the Passover *Haggadah*. This he did, however, for many, even as he had praise for the Jewish people, some disagreements with them, as well as fierce personal allies among them. Stanley Levison, an attorney and consultant, loved and advised King for years, raising funds, drafting King's books and articles, offering his management skills to the Movement. This was done essentially pro bono. King had a very strong rabbinic ally and confidant in Abraham Joshua Heschel, one of the outstanding spiritualists of the twentieth century. So many thousands of Jewish activists, mostly anonymous, found their theologies rekindled. Many were beaten or imprisoned; a few were murdered in the muggy darkness of Alabama and Mississippi. In the end, there were vivid parallels between Moses the lawgiver and Martin Luther King the lawmaker.

Neither of these two men went looking for his mission. When God charged Moses to return to Egypt from his quiet life in Midian and to confront Pharaoh about the Hebrew slaves, Moses was sure that he was the wrong man for the job: "But they will not listen to me, or hearken unto my voice." Moses lacked confidence, nor was he particularly ambitious for the assignment. He even pleaded that he was ill-suited to both confront the Egyptians and inspire the Hebrews, because of a physical impediment: "Oh Lord, I am not a man of words . . . for I am slow of speech and of a slow tongue." Aaron was given the role of spokesman, and Moses emerged as the moral center of the original freedom movement.

It should be noted that Moses never really lived among his own people, the Hebrews. In the biblical story, he was a Hebrew child who serendipitously grew up in the plush environment of the Egyptian palace. He was spared the government's infanticide of Hebrew children and actually became a prince—but grew conflicted about his heritage. He ultimately identified with his true kinsmen, the slaves, and fled Egypt for Midian—after abruptly slaying a taskmaster who had been brutally beating a slave. Like M. L. King of the twentieth century, Moses had legal problems because of his spiritual conflict with profane laws.

Martin Luther King, Jr., scion of a middle-class Atlanta family, namesake and son of a respected preacher, also grew up somewhat removed from the experience of his fellow Southern blacks. Intellectually lithe, worldly, and cultivated, he excelled in graduate studies at Boston University. He earned his doctorate in an environment that few blacks—even as brilliant as him—knew or even understood in the years following World War II. But, like Moses, he was unable to disassociate himself from the tribulations of his people. Feeling a natural affinity, he took on a modest pulpit in Montgomery. He chose a simple lifestyle, an unadorned house, and he desired to preach the Gospel to regular people who brought their prayers, their milestones, and their heartaches to the Dexter Avenue Baptist Church. The great modern scholar Michael Eric Dyson, biographer of both Malcolm X and King, wrote about the preacher: "He was all too aware of his human frailty and had enormous guilt about his worldwide fame."

However, like the modest Moses, the exigencies of society brought King his destiny as well. Montgomery, like all Southern cities in the 1950s, was officially and vociferously segregated. King was offended and angered, although until Rosa Parks sparked the 1955 bus boycott, he remained focused on his ministry. He was all of twenty-six years old. Like Moses, he tended to his family and his flock. He sought only to be a shepherd, but a combination of factors changed King's direction and that of the nation.

I saw a recreation of the bus in which Rosa Parks sat down during my visit to the National Civil Rights Museum in Memphis. I also walked through the actual vehicle, which is on display at the Ford Museum in Dearborn, Michigan.

At the time, the young preacher King was called on to lead the risky confrontation with the Montgomery city government, which was steeped in segregation, racism, and cronyism. A movement, and its leader, was created. King was truly reluctant, paraphrasing Moses' plea that "They won't listen to me. Who am I?" But he was chosen, by fate, by demons, by the winds of time, to become the modern Moses. He would live thirteen more years.

I have spent my entire adult life looking for people who actually knew King and spoke with him, even as I missed him in some odd personal way when I awoke in a fearful sweat on April 5, 1968, in my Cincinnati bedroom. There was Arthur Grant of Toronto, whose family was in the thick of the Canadian human rights movement in the 1950s and 1960s. Arthur was a boy when Dr. King visited the Grant home in the Forest Hills section of Toronto, prior to one of the reverend's stopovers at the Holy Blossom Temple. "What was he like?" I asked Arthur, who served the Reform Jewish association in Canada and the United States for many years before his own untimely death in 2003. I was mesmerized by the notion of Martin Luther King in my friend's house, washing his hands, sharing in the meal, adjusting his seat, making quiet conversation (the great trumpet of a voice lowered to accommodate a dining parlor), excusing himself to use the restroom.

"Unassuming and shy," Arthur told me. "He didn't make a big fuss over himself."

There was Dr. Joan Campbell, the one-time general secretary of the National Council of Churches, who related a story to me about M. L. King while we both appeared on a Cleveland podium for an MLK Day Convocation.

"We were expecting him one afternoon for a dedication ceremony of some kind. This was in the mid-sixties. My doorbell rang at home. Outside in the rain stood a rather small young man, alone in a raincoat. He said, 'Hi, I'm Mike King.' He apologized profusely because he had a cold. He needed some attention, and I warmed him up with some soup and some cough medicine. He was just so humble."

This scene, having taken place in a Shaker Heights, Ohio, home—in the same community where my two daughters grew up—has never left me. The humanity of it, and the tenderness of it, fills me with curiosity and envy. How I would have liked to have given Mike King something warm to eat, and to just chat with him about the rain, children, life itself! This recollection of Dr. Campbell—how it stands in juxtaposition to the untold times that Dr. King was subjected to blows, insults, expulsions, and the cold soup of prison.

My longtime friend Congressman Louis Stokes, one-time chairman of the Congressional Black Caucus as well as the House Select Committee on Assassinations, remembers a telling moment with Martin Luther King. Louis's brother, Carl, was elected mayor of Cleveland in November 1967—during my watershed tenth-grade year with Clifton at Woodward High School. As already noted, Carl was the first African American to ever be elected mayor of a major American city. King was in Cleveland for the tight balloting and shared an upstairs conference room with the Stokes brothers in a downtown building on election night. When word came that Carl had won the mayoralty, he had to go downstairs to meet the press and accept the results. According to Louis Stokes, Carl invited Dr. King to join him at the podium. King politely declined, saying: "If I go down there with you, people will be looking at me and this should be all about you." Brother Louis was not comfortable just leaving MLK by himself, so he spent a long interval chatting privately with King in the room while Carl went down to accept the historic election outcome.

David Garrow, the eminent biographer of King, does offer a different account of this episode in his landmark book *Bearing the Cross*. Garrow writes that King "spent Election day visiting bars and shopping areas, urging people to go to the polls." That night, asserts Garrow, "King waited in his hotel room for a call inviting him to join the new mayor on the platform at the victory party. The call never came . . ." Garrow concedes that the "rebuff" might have been accidental. Six months before his assassination in Memphis, Dr. King was all too frequently seen as a lightning rod for controversy or even failure, even by some of his black brothers. History shows that he was a momentous success, and that his legacy, though sometimes debated or skewed, is one of Mosaic proportions. Whatever happened that night in Cleveland, King was modest, self-effacing, and it is comforting to honor my friend Louis Stokes's recollection of the man who helped break the color line among America's mayors.

And so, lifted by my Woodward years, I have sought to draw upon my experiences and relationships to learn everything possible from people who touched, spoke to, and even held Dr. Martin Luther King, Jr. No treasure in this category has been greater than the personal discussion I had in early 2007 with Reverend Samuel "Billy" Kyles of Memphis.

Dr. King completed his personal analogy to Moses on the storm-tossed and prophetic night of April 3, 1968—when he declaimed his immortal "I've Been to the Mountaintop" speech at the Mason Temple in Memphis. Billy Kyles, King's comrade, who would wrap the martyred reverend in an orange blanket the next evening at the Lorraine Motel, told me about the "Mountaintop" oration. "Yes, Martin preached the fear of death out of himself that night. He wasn't supposed to even be there. He was exhausted, and Ralph (Abernathy) was going to speak. But the crowd wanted Martin, so Ralph called him and he came over.

"Martin had always been afraid of being killed. That night, we had a terrible storm. Rain was pounding on the roof, and the rafters shook with the thunder and lightning. I remember: The thunderclaps and the wind sent the windows banging. Each time it happened, Martin flinched. He was sure someone was lurking and going to shoot him. But when he got to the end of that speech and told us he had looked over and seen the Promised Land, a great calm came over him. Everyone was transfixed. He was freed from his fear and actually he was telling all of us that it would be all right. When he finished speaking, he almost fell into our arms. He was bathed in sweat but you could see relief in his face.

"The next day, he was so playful. I hadn't seen him so happy in years. He was carefree, kidding everybody. When Andy (Young) came back from court in the afternoon, he started that pillow fight. He was teasing me about my new house, saying it was too fancy for a simple preacher. He teased me about dinner, which we were going to have at my house that evening. He said it'd better be real soul food, good food, or he'd tell everybody I couldn't deliver. He was happy."

Dr. Martin Luther King, Jr. was on his way to Reverend Billy Kyles's home for dinner at 6 P.M. on Thursday evening, April 4, 1968. He stood on the balcony of the Lorraine Motel and took in the cool air. A single bullet knocked him down with terrible force. Billy Kyles, Ralph Abernathy, Andrew Young, and the others gathered around him, trying to comprehend the pool of blood. None of these men, including their fallen Moses, was even forty years old.

In Cincinnati, Clifton Fleetwood and I absorbed the news in separate homes and separate worlds. We would cross paths the next morning across the front lawn of our high school, suddenly strangers in our friendship, both of our lives altered in ways that didn't become clear for many years. The high school would become a cultural frontier that will always beguile us but never leave us, as in the words of the old oath recited by both Clifton Fleetwood and me:

> I PLEDGE MY HEART,
> MY HEAD, MY HAND,
> AND BID THEE GODSPEED, WOODWARD.

Lightning, Forty Years Later

n the spring of 2008, with a turbulent campaign in full swing for the Democratic presidential nomination, many people speculated about Barack Obama's middle name. An archconservative and antagonistic radio talk-show host on WLW Radio in Cincinnati embarrassed the eventual Republican nominee, Senator John McCain, during the days leading up to the crucial Ohio primary on March 4. The announcer, while introducing the senator at a rally at the University of Cincinnati, repetitively referred derisively to "Barack HUSSEIN Obama." "How can we have a president named 'Barack HUSSEIN Obama'?" McCain took some responsibility for the overzealous and incendiary act, roundly condemning such pandering the same day.

This, of course, wasn't all that different from charges planted in the media by the campaign of Senator Hillary Rodham Clinton that Obama was actually a Muslim. A photograph of Senator Obama—the first black American to become an extremely serious contender for the presidency—appeared: he was dressed in the turban and garb of his African heritage, clothed as a Somali elder during a visit in August 2006 to Wajir, a rural area in northeastern Kenya near the borders with Somalia and Ethiopia. The racism and the fear-mongering were all part of the cultural zeitgeist that trailed the brilliant young man whose mellifluous tones and stirring words of hope and reconciliation recalled the cadence of M. L. King and the all-too-brief 1968 presidential ballad of Robert F. Kennedy.

The irony was that while some focused on Obama's middle name (and even made insidious charges that he had sworn his senatorial oath on the Koran), nobody seemed to mention his first name. Barack, in Hebrew, means "lightning." As the senator won so many primaries that winter and spring, I called my old friend and Woodward walking mate Steve back in Cincinnati time and again. He was now a veteran reporter and analyst for the PBS radio station in Cincinnati and was closely covering the presidential campaign. He joined the press corps that interviewed Senators McCain, Clinton, and Obama on the same day in Cincinnati. He was present in the hall when the WLW host made a mockery of the introduction of McCain.

We had endured so much together as fifteen-year-olds in 1968, including the assassinations, the Vietnam bloodshed, the urban riots, the explosive Democratic convention in Chicago that—minus Bobby—nominated the party standard, Vice President Hubert Humphrey. We had walked to Woodward High School day in and day out, both exhilarated and afraid, as our American world recoiled in conflict—and the one thing we could have never imagined in the spring of 1968, as King was buried in Atlanta and Bobby next to his brother in Arlington, Virginia, was that lightning would appear within our lifetimes, and that a black man would contend with a white woman as the two finalists for the Democratic presidential nomination.

Even Louis Stokes was having an emotional time, as lightning flashed across the national sky. A few days before the Ohio primary, I reached the former congressman in Cleveland. We had worked together so closely for so long in Ohio and in Washington. I had been his personal guest on the White

House lawn on the brilliant sunny day in September 1993 when Prime Minister Yitzhak Rabin of Israel and Palestinian chairman Yasir Arafat (both since deceased, Rabin assassinated) shook hands and signed the Declaration of Principles. President Bill Clinton may have pulled the two men together a bit on the podium, but they shook hands nonetheless.

Louis Stokes and I wept together, that hot day on the South Lawn—as did many of the three thousand guests, ambassadors, parliamentarians, diplomats, dignitaries, and soldiers. Men and women of every known color and creed, garb, flourish, culture, language, and ethnicity caught a collective breath as the two ingrained enemies shook hands. Wild applause broke out and echoed against the White House walls; I put my head into Lou Stokes's big shoulders and there I was, for an instant, marching down the halls of Woodward High School again, banging on the bass drum, keeping in step with the wiry Clifton Fleetwood, who twirled his baton and shook his feet in a glee and freedom that transcended every set of chains set to be imposed upon us.

Now, fifteen years after the faded hopes of the Oslo accords signed that day, forty years after Memphis, lightning flashed across America in 2008. So many things we had been told in high school were being thrown out. Forty years after Bobby Kennedy's refrain of "We can do better," and Dr. King's intonation, "I may not get there with you, but I want you to know tonight that we as a people will get to the Promised Land," Louis Stokes spoke to me over the telephone.

"I tell you, Ben. I remember, Carl and I used to talk it over back in the sixties when he was mayor of Cleveland and I was going into Congress. It was so hard for him to win that race in '67. There was so much hate. But there he was, the first black man to become mayor of any big city. But still we thought, will we ever see a black man really running for president in our lifetimes?" My friend's sentiment was palpable, and I heard the painful cry of history being released, like a millstone, across the phone lines. Suddenly, it wasn't all in vain, the shootings of Medgar Evers, Malcolm X, Martin King, and so many others whose names are only known to God. Suddenly, it wasn't about the superficial and financially driven plethora of brand-name black athletes selling deodorants, cars, sneakers, beer, and pension portfolios on television. It wasn't window-dressing or affirmative action or quota-filling. It was real, thrilling, and though it was a political campaign, it was ultimately dignified, and it smacked of reconciliation, and it proved that in America, forty years after time stopped on the Lorraine Motel balcony, lightning flashed across the plains and the mountains with the incandescence of hope. Barack Obama was not really the first one to declare, "Yes, we can." But he was the first one with black skin to say it, and to win a whole lot of presidential primaries and caucuses.

Race was back, center stage, even as the official MLK memorial was being built in Washington—adjacent to those of Jefferson and Lincoln. My two adult daughters, in their mid-twenties, were engaged in the Obama campaign; they had grown up with my stories of Clifton Fleetwood, Dr. King, and the Stokes brothers of Cleveland. The congressman was present at their bat mitzvah ceremonies and other milestones. Their high school, the lauded Shaker Heights High School, was a second-generation Woodward model—without the prevalence of racial tension and violence, and with a strong community tradition of multiculturalism. They attended the funerals of the parents of their black classmates, and they stood with me, and the Stokes family, when I helped dedicate the Shaker Heights Post Office in the name of Louise Stokes—mother of Louis and Carl—in 2000.

"This kid, Obama, he's got something," Louis Stokes said to me, his voice cracking as we spoke in March 2008.

For my stepchildren, in their teens during the fortieth anniversary of Dr. King's assassination, there was no discernible race issue. They understood and honored the jubilation people like me felt in the *meaning* of Barack Obama's remarkable candidacy, but to everyone's benefit, really, they didn't quite get what the big deal was. In that polite default of theirs was a fulfillment of Dr. King's words at the Lincoln Memorial in August 1963: "I have a dream . . . that one day my children will be judged not by the color of their skin, but by the content of their character." My stepkids in 2008 were sending text messages and interfacing on MySpace with black kids, Asian, Muslim, Jewish, Latino—they had no rainbow, just the sky itself.

It was not all harmony, and it never will be. What started in the Bible—that is, human prejudice and the proclivity to violence—will never end. There was still a beastly war to protest, forty years after Vietnam. Nooses appeared on college campuses and in city squares—a most grisly reminder of the deepest Southern tradition of racial contempt. The economic gap in America remained an indictment of America's fairness doctrine, and it cut across racial lines, and an elderly Martin Luther King would have spoken and written about this postmodern version of national discrimination. He would have only been seventy-nine in 2008, and would have called us to distinguish between the security of our border and our plain old insecurity about brown immigrants.

He would have smiled, however, at the 2007 Super Bowl. Two African American coaches, Tony Dungy of the Indianapolis Colts and Lovie Smith of the Chicago Bears, squared off in the championship of professional football. It was a first—another step on the civil rights journey that appeared not to be made, and bled, in vain. He would certainly have smiled at Barack Obama; the thunder and lightning that made him wince at the Mason Temple in Memphis on the night of April 3, 1968, finally given way to fresh light and happy noise.

· · · · ·

After a second, not-as-extended search for his new number, I reached Clifton Fleetwood in the spring of 2008. The catering business was doing reasonably well, and he still lived in his late mother's home. "Most of my friends lost whatever homes they got," he mentioned. "They telling us that the economy is still okay, but nobody can keep a house and nobody can drive their cars too much because who's got almost four dollars for a gallon? That ain't right, Ben."

Woodward High School's old building had been completely torn down, he told me. I felt a strange sense of relief—too much that was too old and too wrong had happened among those walls, and the good parts were rising in other forms across the landscape of our now middle-aged existence. Even Barack Obama had only been a child when M. L. King walked the nation, trying to create, well, that very kind of lightning.

"What about Obama and all that, Clifton? What do you think?"

"This is for us," my friend answered.

Bibliography

Branch, Taylor. *Pillar of Fire: America in the King Years 1963–65*. New York: Touchstone, 1998.

———. *At Canaan's Edge: America in the King Years 1965–68*. New York: Simon and Schuster, 2006.

Carson, Clayborne, ed. *The Autobiography of Martin Luther King*. New York: Warner Books, 1998.

Dyson, Michael Eric. *I May Not Get There With You: The True Martin Luther King, Jr.* New York: Touchstone, 2000.

———. *April 4, 1968: Martin Luther King's Death and How It Changed America*. New York: Basic Civitas Books, 2008.

Frady, Marshall. *Martin Luther King, Jr.* New York: Viking, 2002.

Frank, Gerold. *An American Death: The True Story of the Assassination of Martin

Luther King, Jr., and the Greatest Manhunt of Our Time. Garden City, NY: Doubleday and Company, 1972.

Garrow, David. *Bearing the Cross: Martin Luther King, Jr., and the Southern Christian Leadership Conference.* New York: William Morrow and Company, 1986.

Hamill, Pete. *PieceWork: Writings on Men and Women, Fools and Heroes, Lost Cities, Vanished Friends, Small Pleasures, Large Calamities, and How the Weather Was.* Boston: Little, Brown and Company, 1996.

Haskins, Jim. *The Day Martin Luther King, Jr. Was Shot: A Photo History of the Civil Rights Movement.* New York: Scholastic, Inc., 1992.

Johnson, Charles, and Bob Adelman. *King: The Photobiography of Martin Luther King, Jr.* New York: Penguin Putnam, Inc., 2000.

Kamin, Ben. *Thinking Passover: A Rabbi's Book of Holiday Values.* New York: Dutton, 1997.

Kennedy, Caroline, ed. *A Patriot's Handbook: Songs, Poems, Stories, and Speeches Celebrating the Land We Love.* New York: Hyperion, 2003.

King, Coretta Scott, ed. *The Words of Martin Luther King, Jr.* New York: Newmarket Press, 1983, 1987.

King, Martin Luther, Jr. *Where Do We Go from Here: Chaos or Community?* Boston: Beacon Press, 1967.

Kotz, Nick. *Judgment Days: Lyndon Johnson, Martin Luther King, Jr., and the Laws That Changed America.* Boston and New York: Houghton Mifflin Company, 2005.

Kurlansky, Mark. *1968: The Year That Rocked the World.* New York: Ballantine Books, 2004.

Lewis, John. *Walking with the Wind: A Memoir of the Movement.* New York: Simon and Schuster, 1998.

O'Neill, William L. *Coming Apart: An Informal History of America in the 1960's.* Chicago: Quadrangle Books, 1971.

Posner, Gerald. *Killing the Dream: James Earl Ray and the Assassination of Martin Luther King, Jr.* New York: Random House, 1998.

Roberts, Gene, and Hank Klibanoff. *The Race Beat: The Press, the Civil Rights Struggle, and the Awakening of a Nation*. New York: Alfred A. Knopf, 2006.

Rowan, Cart T. *Dream Makers, Dream Breakers: The World of Justice Thurgood Marshall*. Boston: Little, Brown and Company, 1993.

Salzman, Jack, ed. *Bridges and Boundaries: African Americans and American Jews*. New York: George Braziller, Inc., and The Jewish Museum, 1992.

Shatzkin, Mike, and Jim Charlton, eds. *The Ballplayers*. New York: Arbor House, 1990.

Talbot, David. *Brothers: The Hidden History of the Kennedy Years*. New York: The Free Press, 2007.

Woodward, C. Vann. *The Burden of Southern History*. Baton Rouge: Louisiana State University Press, 1960.

Acknowledgments

More than forty years ago, a group of literate, creative, and high-spirited students at Woodward High School in Cincinnati collaborated on and produced a comprehensive, hardback school annual aptly called *Woodward Treasures*. I did not know them all, and they have gone on to lives and careers and far-flung places. Sadly, a few have already passed on. The 1968 *Treasures* was so rich with ideas, imagery, and design—and so dramatically reflective of those times—that it won an award as the finest high school yearbook in America. This memoir could not have been written without the information, reflections, and the context provided to me by the unsung varsity journalists of the *Treasures* editions 1968, 1969, and 1970. The student editor of that landmark 1968 edition was Ian Smith, and the faculty advisor was Jack Luhrman. I thank them, and their colleagues, in my heart.

Martha Bates, acquisitions editor at Michigan State University Press, and the editor of this book, has become an exquisite friend. She believed in this project as much as she believes that something indelible happened in America in the 1960s, and that Martin Luther King, Jr., was a man who defied any category. Dr. King taught people like Martha Bates and me that the measure of life is the ability to ask painful questions.

I am so grateful to Clifton Fleetwood, my classmate, barometer, and spiritual touchstone for some forty years. I acknowledge with deep affection my walking schoolmate and lifelong chum Steve Hirschberg, who is a central character, not only in this memoir but in so many stories I have published about our shared experiences.

Congressman Louis Stokes, a personal hero to me, and a genuine friend, with whom I have cowritten articles, wept, and laughed boisterously, remains an inspiration to me in the matter of black/white relations and the meaning of this American civilization.

My adult daughters, Sari and Debra, grew up listening to me, wittingly or not, telling the stories of Clifton Fleetwood, M. L. King, the Kennedys, and human rights, and have never lost patience with my love of history—and a now-vanished high school that was the house of history. When it comes to my absolute need to write this book, they get it.

Audrey, my wife, best friend, kindred spirit, muse, personal editor, and primal advocate, is more responsible than anybody else for my opportunity to realize this dream.

Thank you, Dr. King, for ordaining me into my own kind of ministry.